P9-DEZ-342

Spelling
Handbook

Book Staff and Contributors

Marianne Murphy   *Content Specialist*
David Shireman   *Instructional Designer*
Mary Beck Desmond   *Senior Text Editor*
Ron Stanley   *Text Editor*
Suzanne Montazer   *Creative Director, Print and ePublishing*
Sasha Blanton   *Senior Print Visual Designer*
Julie Jankowski, Eric Trott   *Print Visual Designers*
Stephanie Williams   *Cover Designer*
Tim Mansfield   *Writer*
Amy Eward   *Senior Manager, Writers*
Susan Raley   *Manager, Editors*
Colleen Line   *Senior Project Manager*

Maria Szalay   *Senior Vice President for Product Development*
John Holdren   *Senior Vice President for Content and Curriculum*
David Pelizzari   *Vice President, Content and Curriculum*
Kim Barcas   *Vice President, Creative*
Laura Seuschek   *Vice President, Instructional Design and Evaluation & Research*
Aaron Hall   *Vice President, Program Management*

Lisa Dimaio Iekel   *Production Manager*
John Agnone   *Director of Publications*

About K12 Inc.

K12 Inc., a technology-based education company, is the nation's leading provider of proprietary curriculum and online education programs to students in grades K–12. K12 provides its curriculum and academic services to online schools, traditional classrooms, blended school programs, and directly to families. K12 Inc. also operates the K12 International Academy, an accredited, diploma-granting online private school serving students worldwide. K12's mission is to provide any child the curriculum and tools to maximize success in life, regardless of geographic, financial, or demographic circumstances. K12 Inc. is accredited by CITA. More information can be found at www.K12.com.

978-1-60153-174-2
Printed by RR Donnelley & Sons, Roanoke, VA, USA, May 2015

Contents

K¹² Spelling Course Overview

Overview

My spelling is Wobbly. It's good spelling but it Wobbles, and the letters get in the wrong places. — **A. A. Milne**

The goal of K¹² Spelling is to ensure students don't wobble with their spelling the way Winnie-the-Pooh does. As an engaging, portable program that can be tailored to the individual needs of students, K¹² Spelling will help students master the conventions of spelling needed to be proficient readers and writers.

While many may wonder about the need for formal spelling instruction in the digital age, K¹² firmly believes in the power and necessity of mastering the traditional subject of spelling. K¹² Spelling focuses on learning to recognize patterns rather than memorizing rules—no spelling rule is 100 percent reliable. Research shows that good readers and spellers do not decode (read) and encode (spell) rules, but rather letter patterns that help them identify words and differentiate one word from another.

A great deal of research shows that continually revisiting and building on mastered concepts helps students master new concepts. With each subsequent grade level, spelling conventions build on previously mastered content while giving students many options for multimodal learning. Throughout grades 1–5, students build a strong foundation that leads to a strong storehouse of knowledge about spelling and the English language.

K¹² Spelling is designed to accommodate students who will master the content at different paces and who will require varying amounts of study. K¹² believes that students can learn to spell words quickly by studying spelling patterns that are common to many words. A certain number of common words fall outside these conventions, and students need to learn to spell those words quickly in preparation for the demands of grade-level writing requirements.

To balance the goals of learning to spell both within and outside spelling conventions, the spelling words in K¹² Spelling are divided into four categories: Heart Words, Target Words, Challenge Words, and Alternate Words.

Heart Words represent some of the most commonly spelled words outside the spelling conventions taught at each grade level. Other programs may refer to these as sight words, trick words, or snap words. Heart Words do not follow the spelling patterns being covered in the unit, but it is important for students to learn to spell these very common words that have to be learned "by heart." A unit will typically include two to four Heart Words. You will help students track which Heart Words they have mastered, and students will continue to study each Heart Word until they have mastered it. All students are expected to demonstrate mastery of Heart Words.

Target Words follow the spelling pattern being studied in a unit. For example, all Target Words for a given unit may be words that end with a double letter. Along with the Heart Words, these words represent the core content to be learned by students in a unit. A unit will present ten Target Words. All students are expected to demonstrate mastery of Target Words.

Challenge Words also follow the spelling convention being studied in any given unit, but are somewhat more difficult to spell. Challenge Words will be presented to students only if they first show mastery of the unit's Heart Words and Target Words. Each unit includes two to four Challenge Words. Not all students are expected to demonstrate mastery of Challenge Words.

Alternate Words are like Target Words and represent another set of words that follow the spelling convention being studied in the unit. Alternate Words are a source of extra words for students who show ready mastery of the Heart Words and Target Words. Ten Alternate Words are identified in most units. Not all students are expected to demonstrate mastery of Alternate Words.

Unit Plans

K[12] Spelling presents a cohesive, pattern-based program designed to enable you to guide students through the instruction of these four different types of words.

K[12] Spelling Purple consists of 36 units. Each five-day unit focuses on a particular spelling convention and follows a set, repeated pattern.

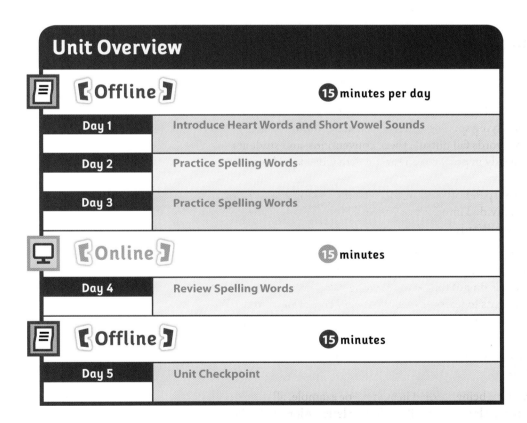

Unit Overview		
Offline		**15** minutes per day
Day 1	Introduce Heart Words and Short Vowel Sounds	
Day 2	Practice Spelling Words	
Day 3	Practice Spelling Words	
Online		**15** minutes
Day 4	Review Spelling Words	
Offline		**15** minutes
Day 5	Unit Checkpoint	

Day 1

On Day 1, students' spelling list, or Words to Learn, is determined. Students will take a pretest, establishing their initial level of mastery of the spelling words presented in that unit. You will then guide students through the discovery of the spelling convention being studied in that unit, and students will briefly practice the spelling words that they did not master in the pretest.

Day 2

You will use the Activity Bank to practice spelling words with students. The Activity Bank is a collection of interactive, offline activities designed to allow students to practice spelling words in a variety of ways. You can choose any of the activities in the Activity Bank to do on Days 2 and 3 of the unit, so try out as many of the activities as possible to discover which ones motivate and produce the best learning for your students.

Day 3

You will use the Activity Bank to practice spelling words with students. You are encouraged, but not required, to choose activities different from those you used on Day 2.

Day 4

Students will play an online game in which they review the spelling words in the unit. At the beginning of the game, you will choose whether the game should present only the Heart Words and Target Words to students, or whether Challenge Words or Alternate Words should also be included. This online review serves as preparation for the assessment (Unit Checkpoint) on Day 5.

Day 5

Students will complete an offline Unit Checkpoint covering the words from their Words to Learn list. You will enter the results of the assessment online to track student progress.

Since each unit follows the same pattern, full activity directions for each day will be repeated only in the first two Unit Plans. In subsequent units, an abbreviated version of the instructions is presented. However, the spelling words, materials lists, advance preparation, and any guidance particular to a unit will be presented in each specific Unit Plan.

Review Units

Every sixth unit in K[12] Spelling is a review unit. Review units consist of the same introduction, practice, and assessment procedures as other units. But instead of introducing a new spelling convention, they review the spelling conventions studied in the previous five units. In the review unit, all the Heart Words from the previous five units are presented, and the Target Words are made up of a selection of words from previous units representing each of the spelling conventions covered. The Challenge Words and Alternate Words are new words that also represent the spelling conventions studied in the previous five units.

Spelling Handbook

Heart Words and Short Vowel Sounds

Target spelling convention — one vowel + one or more consonants

Short vowel sounds are usually spelled with one vowel followed by one or more consonants. Each of this unit's Target Words contains a short vowel sound spelled this way.

Unit Overview

📋 **〔Offline〕**		🕐 **minutes per day**
Day 1	Introduce Heart Words and Short Vowel Sounds	
Day 2	Practice Spelling Words	
Day 3	Practice Spelling Words	
💻 **〔Online〕**		🕐 **minutes**
Day 4	Review Spelling Words	
📋 **〔Offline〕**		🕐 **minutes**
Day 5	Unit Checkpoint	

☁️ **Heart Words**

have	say	hard
may		

⭐ **Challenge Words**

difficult	children	exact

◎ **Target Words**

next	rabbit	pocket
until	magnet	finish
happen	ticket	publish
sudden		

Alternate Words

public	himself	anthem
fantastic	locket	establish
contest	problem	packet
polish		

[Offline] ⏱ minutes per day

Complete the Spelling activities with students.

Day 1 ....

Introduce Heart Words and Short Vowel Sounds

Advance Preparation

Write each Heart, Target, Challenge, and Alternate Word on a separate index card. Use small symbols or letters to indicate which type of word is written on each card. For example, you can use a T for Target Words, a heart symbol for Heart Words, a C for Challenge Words, and an A for Alternate Words.

T shop	♡ a	C suntan	A dock

Pretest

1. Using the index cards you prepared, **say** each Heart and Target Word and have students write it on a whiteboard or sheet of paper. As you give the pretest, place the cards for words students spelled correctly in a Mastered pile. Place the cards for words students misspelled in a Words to Learn pile.

2. **Gather** the cards for all the words students have misspelled, which will be students' Words to Learn for this unit. It is best if students have between 10 and 20 Words to Learn, depending on students' rate of mastery.

   ▸ If students misspelled only a few words, consider adding a few Challenge or Alternate Words.
   ▸ If students didn't misspell any Heart or Target Words, give them a pretest using the Challenge and Alternate Words. Add the words they misspell to their Words to Learn.

Note: If students didn't misspell any Heart, Target, Challenge, or Alternate Words, mark Lessons 2 and 3 complete and move to the online activity for Day 4 to practice for the Unit Checkpoint on Day 5.

Heart Words

Heart Words do not follow spelling conventions, so we learn them "by heart."

⟳ *Skip this activity if students didn't misspell any Heart Words on this unit's pretest.*

1. **Gather** the Words to Learn cards for any Heart Words.

2. **Practice** the Heart Words.

   ▸ Have students choose a card and read the word aloud.

   Successful?
   - Cover the card and have students write it on a whiteboard or sheet of paper.
   - Go to the next word.

   Not successful?
   - Say the word and have students spell it aloud.
   - Have students picture the letters of the word in their mind.
   - Have students write the word again on a whiteboard or sheet of paper.
   - Have students spell the word aloud again.
   - Continue this way through all the Heart Words for this unit.

3. **Track mastery** of Heart Words.

   ▸ When students read and spell a Heart Word correctly, mark the index card with the date.
   ▸ When any index card has three dates marked on it, that card should be moved from the group of Heart Words students are still working on to the group of Heart Words students have mastered.

Target Words

Target Words have the single spelling convention we're focusing on in this lesson.

⟳ *Skip this activity if students didn't misspell any Target Words on this unit's pretest.*

1. **Gather** the Words to Learn cards for any Target Words.

2. **Discover** the new spelling convention.

   ▸ Explain the new spelling convention described at the beginning of this unit.
   ▸ Have students search for the new spelling convention in the words on the index cards.
   ▸ Say and discuss the new spelling convention in each Target Word.
   ▸ Have students picture the letters of the word in their minds.

3. **Practice** the Target Words.

   ▸ Have students sound out the Target Words.
   ▸ Have students point out the spelling convention in the words.
   ▸ Say a word and have students spell it aloud.

Successful?

- Go to the next word.

Not successful?

- Review the correct spelling with students.
- Have students write the word on a whiteboard or sheet of paper.
- Have students spell the word aloud again.

► Continue this way through all the Target Words for this unit.

Challenge Words

Challenge Words follow the unit's spelling convention, but are more difficult than the Target Words.

⮌ *Skip this activity if students are struggling with the Heart Words and Target Words.*

1. **Gather** the Words to Learn cards for any Challenge Words.

2. **Discover** the new spelling convention in the Challenge Words.

   ► Explain the new spelling convention described at the beginning of this unit.
   ► Have students search for the new spelling convention in the words on the index cards.
   ► Say each word and have students spell it aloud.
   ► Have students picture the letters of each word in their mind.

3. **Practice** the Challenge Words.

   ► Have students write the word on a whiteboard or sheet of paper.
   ► Have students spell the word aloud again.

Alternate Words

Alternate Words follow the unit's spelling convention.

⮌ *Skip this activity if students don't have any Words to Learn cards for Alternate Words.*

1. **Gather** the Words to Learn cards for any Alternate Words.

2. **Discover** the new spelling convention in the Alternate Words.

   ► Explain the new spelling convention described at the beginning of this unit.
   ► Have students search for the new spelling convention in the words on the index cards.
   ► Say each word and have students spell it aloud.
   ► Have students picture the letters of each word in their mind.

3. **Practice** the Alternate Words.

   ► Have students write the word on a whiteboard or sheet of paper.
   ► Have students spell the word aloud again.

Practice Spelling Words

Students need to practice only the words on their Words to Learn cards from Day 1.

1. **Choose** a spelling activity from the Activity Bank.

2. **Use** all the Words to Learn during the activity.

3. **Choose** a second activity if you have time.

Practice Spelling Words

Follow the same procedure as on Day 2, but choose different activities from the Activity Bank.

 **15 minutes**

Review Spelling Words

Help students **find the online review activity**, choose Challenge Words or Alternate Words if students have studied those words in this unit, and provide support as needed.

[Offline] 15 minutes

Day 5

Unit Checkpoint

Students will complete an offline Unit Checkpoint covering the words on their Words to Learn list.

1. **Dictate** the Words to Learn.

   ► Have students write the words on a sheet of paper.

2. **Check** students' answers.

   ► Circle the words students spell incorrectly.
   ► Enter students' results online.

3. **Review** the words students misspelled.

   ► Gather these index cards and put them aside for further practice as time allows.

Rewards:

- Help students find and play the online Spelling game, Spell 'n' Stack. Students should use levels 1–3.

- If students scored 80 percent or above on the Unit Checkpoint, add a sticker to the Unit 1 box on students' My Accomplishments chart. If students scored under 80 percent, continue to practice the words that they missed and add a sticker to this unit once they have mastered the words.

Heart Words and Suffixes –s & –es

Target spelling convention — **base word + *s* or *es* to form a plural**

Most nouns can be made plural by adding the suffix –*s* or –*es*. We add the suffix –*es* to words ending in *ch, sh, s, x,* or *z*. The suffix –*s* is added to most other words. All of this unit's Target Words are plurals ending in –*s* or –*es*.

Objectives
- Spell Heart Words.
- Spell plurals ending in –*s* or –*es*.

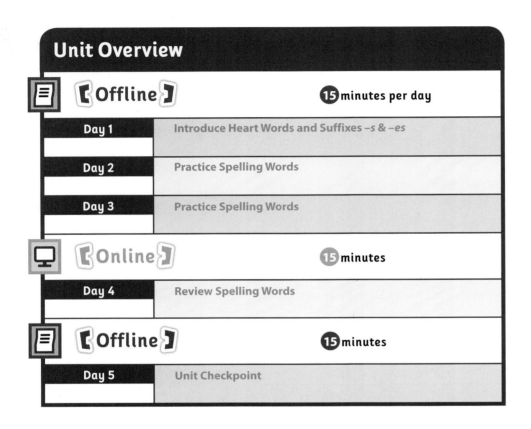

Unit Overview

Offline — 15 minutes per day

Day 1	Introduce Heart Words and Suffixes –s & –es
Day 2	Practice Spelling Words
Day 3	Practice Spelling Words

Online — 15 minutes

| Day 4 | Review Spelling Words |

Offline — 15 minutes

| Day 5 | Unit Checkpoint |

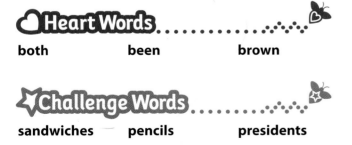

Heart Words

both   been   brown

Challenge Words

sandwiches   pencils   presidents

Target Words

objects	plants	foxes
insects	trucks	riches
facts	napkins	gashes
products		

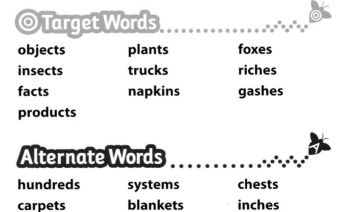

Alternate Words

hundreds	systems	chests
carpets	blankets	inches
numbers	dresses	bunches
lunches		

[Offline] 🕙 minutes per day

Complete the Spelling activities with students.

Introduce Heart Words and Suffixes −s & −es

[Materials]

- index cards (26)
- whiteboard (optional)

Advance Preparation

Write each Heart, Target, Challenge, and Alternate Word on a separate index card. Use small symbols or letters to indicate which type of word is written on each card. For example, you can use a T for Target Words, a heart symbol for Heart Words, a C for Challenge Words, and an A for Alternate Words.

Pretest

1. Using the index cards you prepared, **say** each Heart and Target Word and have students write it on a whiteboard or sheet of paper. As you give the pretest, place the cards for words students spelled correctly in a Mastered pile. Place the cards for words students misspelled in a Words to Learn pile.

2. **Gather** the cards for all the words students have misspelled, which will be students' Words to Learn for this unit. It is best if students have between 10 and 20 Words to Learn, depending on students' rate of mastery.

   ▸ If students misspelled only a few words, consider adding a few Challenge or Alternate Words.
   ▸ If students didn't misspell any Heart or Target Words, give them a pretest using the Challenge and Alternate Words. Add the words they misspell to their Words to Learn.

Note: If students didn't misspell any Heart, Target, Challenge, or Alternate Words, mark Lessons 2 and 3 complete and move to the online activity for Day 4 to practice for the Unit Checkpoint on Day 5.

Heart Words

Heart Words do not follow spelling conventions, so we learn them "by heart."

⮕ *Skip this activity if students didn't misspell any Heart Words on this unit's pretest.*

1. **Gather** the Words to Learn cards for any new Heart Words.

2. **Practice** the *new* Heart Words.

   ▸ Have students choose a card and read the word aloud.

   Successful?
   • Cover the card and have students write it on a whiteboard or sheet of paper.
   • Go to the next word.

   Not successful?
   • Say the word and have students spell it aloud.
   • Have students picture the letters of the word in their mind.
   • Have students write the word again on a whiteboard or sheet of paper.
   • Have students spell the word aloud again.
   • Continue this way through all the new Heart Words for this unit.

3. **Practice** *all* Heart Words.

   ▸ Add the new Heart Words to the Words to Learn cards of all the Heart Words students have not yet mastered.
   ▸ Have students choose a card and read the word aloud.

   Successful?
   • Cover the card and have students write it on a whiteboard or sheet of paper.
   • Go to the next word.

   Not successful?
   • Say the word and have students spell it aloud.
   • Have students picture the letters of the word in their minds.
   • Have students write the word again on a whiteboard or sheet of paper.
   • Have students spell the word aloud again.

   ▸ Continue this way through all Heart Words students have not yet mastered.

4. **Track mastery** of Heart Words.

   ▸ When students read and spell a Heart Word correctly, mark the index card with the date.
   ▸ When any index card has three dates marked on it, that card should be moved from the group of Heart Words students are still working on to the group of Heart Words students have mastered.

Target Words

Target Words have the single spelling convention we're focusing on in this lesson.

⮌ *Skip this activity if students didn't misspell any Target Words on this unit's pretest.*

1. **Gather** the Words to Learn cards for any Target Words.

2. **Discover** the new spelling convention.

   ▸ Explain the new spelling convention described at the beginning of this unit.
   ▸ Have students search for the new spelling convention in the words on the index cards.
   ▸ Say and discuss the new spelling convention in each Target Word.
   ▸ Have students picture the letters of the word in their minds.

3. **Practice** the Target Words.

> ‣ Have students sound out the Target Words.
> ‣ Have students point out the spelling convention in the words.
> ‣ Say a word and have students spell it aloud.

> Successful?
> • Go to the next word.

> Not successful?
> • Review the correct spelling with students.
> • Have students write the word on a whiteboard or sheet of paper.
> • Have students spell the word aloud again.
> • Continue this way through all the Target Words for this unit.

Challenge Words

Challenge Words follow the unit's spelling convention, but are more difficult than the Target Words.

⮌ *Skip this activity if students are struggling with the Heart Words and Target Words.*

1. **Gather** the Words to Learn cards for any Challenge Words.

2. **Discover** the new spelling convention in the Challenge Words.

> ‣ Explain the new spelling convention described at the beginning of this unit.
> ‣ Have students search for the new spelling convention in the words on the index cards.
> ‣ Say each word and have students spell it aloud.
> ‣ Have students picture the letters of each word in their mind.

3. **Practice** the Challenge Words.

> ‣ Have students write the word on a whiteboard or sheet of paper.
> ‣ Have students spell the word aloud again.

Alternate Words

Alternate Words follow the unit's spelling convention

⮌ *Skip this activity if students don't have any Words to Learn cards for Alternate Words.*

1. **Gather** the Words to Learn cards for any Alternate Words.

2. **Discover** the new spelling convention in the Alternate Words.

> ‣ Explain the new spelling convention described at the beginning of this unit.
> ‣ Have students search for the new spelling convention in the words on the index cards.
> ‣ Say each word and have students spell it aloud.
> ‣ Have students picture the letters of each word in their mind.

3. **Practice** the Alternate Words.

> ‣ Have students write the word on a whiteboard or sheet of paper.
> ‣ Have students spell the word aloud again.

Day 2

Practice Spelling Words

Students need to practice only the words on their Words to Learn Cards from Day 1.

1. **Choose** a spelling activity from the Activity Bank.
2. **Use** all the Words to Learn during the activity.
3. **Choose** a second activity if you have time.

Day 3

Practice Spelling Words

Follow the same procedure as on Day 2, but choose different activities from the Activity Bank.

 **15 minutes**

Day 4

Review Spelling Words

Help students **find the online review activity**, choose Challenge Words or Alternate Words if students have studied those words in this unit, and provide support as needed.

[Offline] 🕔 minutes

Day 5

Unit Checkpoint

Students will complete an offline Unit Checkpoint covering the words on their Words to Learn list.

1. **Dictate** the Words to Learn.

   ▸ Have students write the words on a sheet of paper.

2. **Check** students' answers.

   ▸ Circle the words students spell incorrectly.
   ▸ Enter students' results online.

3. **Review** the words students misspelled.

   ▸ Gather these index cards and put them aside for further practice as time allows.

Rewards:

- Help students find and play the online Spelling game, Spell 'n' Stack. Students should use levels 1–3.
- If students scored 80 percent or above on the Unit Checkpoint, add a sticker to the Unit 2 box on students' My Accomplishments chart. If students scored under 80 percent, continue to practice the words that they missed and add a sticker to this unit once they have mastered the words.

Heart Words and –*ng* & –*nk* Words

Target spelling convention — **vowel + *ng* or *nk***

The letter combinations –*ang*, –*ing*, –*ong*, –*ung*, –*ank*, –*ink*, –*onk*, and –*unk* have unique sounds that must be learned as units rather than by identifying and spelling their individual components. Each of this unit's Target Words contains the letter combinations –*ang*, –*ing*, –*ong*, –*ung*, –*ank*, –*ink*, –*onk*, and –*unk*.

Objectives
- Spell Heart Words.
- Spell words ending in –*ang*, –*ing*, –*ong*, or –*ung*.
- Spell words ending in –*ank*, –*ink*, –*onk*, or –*unk*.

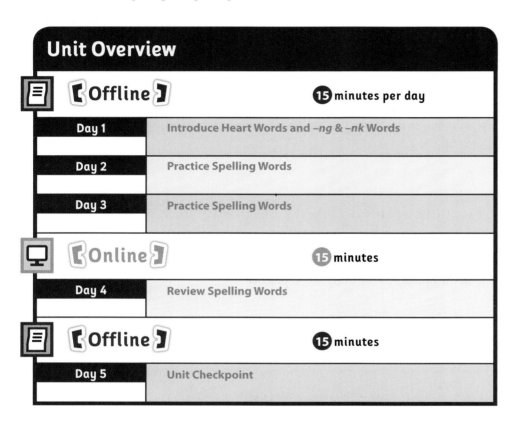

Unit Overview

📋 **[Offline]** 🕐 **15** minutes per day

Day 1	Introduce Heart Words and –*ng* & –*nk* Words
Day 2	Practice Spelling Words
Day 3	Practice Spelling Words

🖥 **[Online]** 🕐 **15** minutes

| Day 4 | Review Spelling Words |

📋 **[Offline]** 🕐 **15** minutes

| Day 5 | Unit Checkpoint |

☁ Heart Words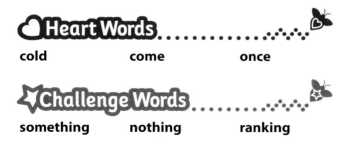

| cold | come | once |

☆ Challenge Words

| something | nothing | ranking |

◎ Target Words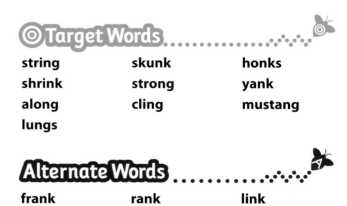

string	skunk	honks
shrink	strong	yank
along	cling	mustang
lungs		

Alternate Words

frank	rank	link
mink	sang	gong
crank	twang	things
clang		

[Offline] ⏱ minutes per day

Complete the Spelling activities with students. **For the full instructions for each activity, refer to pages SP 8–13.**

Day 1

Introduce Heart Words and *–ng* & *–nk* Words

[Materials]

- index cards (26)
- whiteboard (optional)

Advance Preparation

Write each Heart, Target, Challenge, and Alternate Word on a separate index card. Indicate on each card whether a word is a Heart, Target, Challenge, or Alternate Word.

Pretest

1. **Administer** a pretest using the Heart and Target Words.

2. **Gather** students' Words to Learn cards.

Note: If students didn't misspell any Heart, Target, Challenge, or Alternate Words, mark Lessons 2 and 3 complete and move to the online activity for Day 4 to practice for the Unit Checkpoint on Day 5.

Heart Words

➲ *Skip this activity if students didn't misspell any Heart Words on this unit's pretest.*

1. **Gather** the Words to Learn cards for any Heart Words.

2. **Practice** the *new* Heart Words.

3. **Practice** *all* Heart Words.

4. **Track mastery** of Heart Words.

Target Words

➲ *Skip this activity if students didn't misspell any Target Words on this unit's pretest.*

1. **Gather** the Words to Learn cards for any Target Words.

2. **Discover** the new spelling convention.

3. **Practice** the Target Words.

Challenge Words

↪ *Skip this activity if students are struggling with the Heart Words and Target Words.*

1. **Gather** the Words to Learn cards for any Challenge Words.
2. **Discover** the new spelling convention in the Challenge Words.
3. **Practice** the Challenge Words.

Alternate Words

↪ *Skip this activity if students don't have any Words to Learn cards for Alternate Words.*

1. **Gather** the Words to Learn cards for any Alternate Words.
2. **Discover** the new spelling convention in the Alternate Words.
3. **Practice** the Alternate Words.

Day 2

Practice Spelling Words

Practice using the Activity Bank.

Day 3

Practice Spelling Words

Practice using the Activity Bank.

 **15 minutes**

Day 4

Review Spelling Words

Review using the online activity.

[Offline] 🕐 15 minutes

Day 5

Unit Checkpoint

1. **Dictate** the Words to Learn.

2. **Check** students' answers.

3. **Review** the words students misspelled.

Rewards:

- Help students find and play the online Spelling game, Spell 'n' Stack. Students should use levels 1–3.

- If students scored 80 percent or above on the Unit Checkpoint, add a sticker to the Unit 3 box on students' My Accomplishments chart. If students scored under 80 percent, continue to practice the words that they missed and add a sticker to this unit once they have mastered the words.

Heart Words and Long *a* Spellings

Target spelling convention – **letter combinations that create the long *a* sound**

The most common spellings for the long *a* sound are *a*, *ai*, *ay*, *eigh*, and *a*–consonant–*e*. Each of this unit's Target Words contains the long *a* sound spelled with one of these letter combinations.

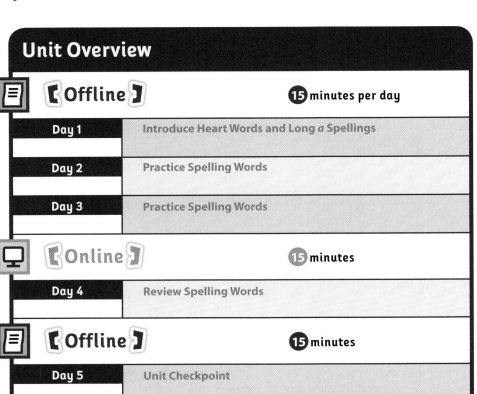

Unit Overview

[Offline]		**15** minutes per day
Day 1	Introduce Heart Words and Long *a* Spellings	
Day 2	Practice Spelling Words	
Day 3	Practice Spelling Words	
[Online]		**15** minutes
Day 4	Review Spelling Words	
[Offline]		**15** minutes
Day 5	Unit Checkpoint	

Heart Words

does	do	done

Challenge Words

neighbor	freight	sleigh

Target Words

later	payment	maintain
always	explain	snail
Sunday	eighteen	lame
holiday		

Alternate Words

basic	awake	weight
dictate	cupcake	pray
label	maze	train
decade		

 **minutes per day**

Complete the Spelling activities with students. **For the full instructions for each activity, refer to pages SP 8–13.**

Introduce Heart Words and Long *a* Spellings

Materials

- index cards (26)
- whiteboard (optional)

Advance Preparation

Write each Heart, Target, Challenge, and Alternate Word on a separate index card. Indicate on each card whether a word is a Heart, Target, Challenge, or Alternate Word.

Pretest

1. **Administer** a pretest using the Heart and Target Words.

2. **Gather** students' Words to Learn cards.

Note: If students didn't misspell any Heart, Target, Challenge, or Alternate Words, mark Lessons 2 and 3 complete and move to the online activity for Day 4 to practice for the Unit Checkpoint on Day 5.

Heart Words

⟳ *Skip this activity if students didn't misspell any Heart Words on this unit's pretest.*

1. **Gather** the Words to Learn cards for any Heart Words.

2. **Practice** the *new* Heart Words.

3. **Practice** *all* Heart Words.

4. **Track mastery** of Heart Words.

Target Words

⟳ *Skip this activity if students didn't misspell any Target Words on this unit's pretest.*

1. **Gather** the Words to Learn cards for any Target Words.

2. **Discover** the new spelling convention.

3. **Practice** the Target Words.

Challenge Words

⮌ *Skip this activity if students are struggling with the Heart Words and Target Words.*

1. **Gather** the Words to Learn cards for any Challenge Words.
2. **Discover** the new spelling convention in the Challenge Words.
3. **Practice** the Challenge Words.

Alternate Words

⮌ *Skip this activity if students don't have any Words to Learn cards for Alternate Words.*

1. **Gather** the Words to Learn cards for any Alternate Words.
2. **Discover** the new spelling convention in the Alternate Words.
3. **Practice** the Alternate Words.

Day 2

Practice Spelling Words

Practice using the Activity Bank.

Day 3

Practice Spelling Words

Practice using the Activity Bank.

 **15** minutes

Day 4

Review Spelling Words

Review using the online activity.

〖 Offline 〗 ⏱ 15 minutes

Day 5

Unit Checkpoint

1. **Dictate** the Words to Learn.

2. **Check** students' answers.

3. **Review** the words students misspelled.

Rewards:

- Help students find and play the online Spelling game, Spell 'n' Stack. Students should use levels 1–3.

- If students scored 80 percent or above on the Unit Checkpoint, add a sticker to the Unit 4 box on students' My Accomplishments chart. If students scored under 80 percent, continue to practice the words that they missed and add a sticker to this unit once they have mastered the words.

Heart Words and Long *i* Spellings

Target spelling convention — letter combinations that create the long *i* sound

The most common spellings for the long *i* sound are *i, ie, igh, y,* and *i*-consonant-*e*. Each of this unit's Target Words contains the long *i* sound spelled with one of these letter combinations.

Objectives

- Spell Heart Words.
- Spell words containing the long *i* sound spelled *i, ie, igh, y,* or *i*-consonant-*e*.

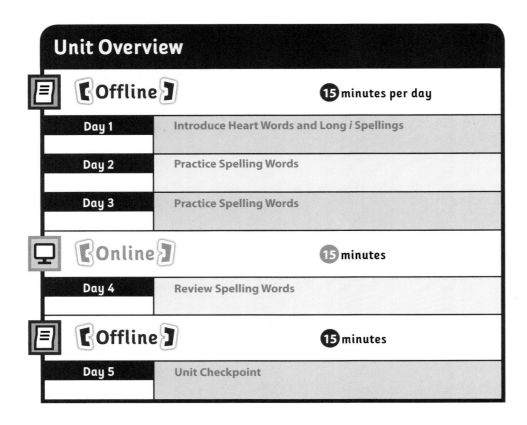

Unit Overview

Offline		15 minutes per day
Day 1	Introduce Heart Words and Long *i* Spellings	
Day 2	Practice Spelling Words	
Day 3	Practice Spelling Words	

Online		15 minutes
Day 4	Review Spelling Words	

Offline		15 minutes
Day 5	Unit Checkpoint	

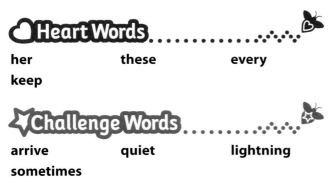

Heart Words

her	these	every
keep		

Challenge Words

arrive	quiet	lightning
sometimes		

Target Words

silent	supply	sigh
kind	why	inside
tie	while	quite
lie		

Alternate Words

entire	apply	line
tight	blind	necktie
child	fry	right

 **15** minutes per day

Complete the Spelling activities with students. **For the full instructions for each activity, refer to pages SP 8–13.**

Day 1

Introduce Heart Words and Long *i* Spellings

- index cards (27)
- whiteboard (optional)

Advance Preparation

Write each Heart, Target, Challenge, and Alternate Word on a separate index card. Indicate on each card whether a word is a Heart, Target, Challenge, or Alternate Word.

Pretest

1. **Administer** a pretest using the Heart and Target Words.

2. **Gather** students' Words to Learn cards.

Note: If students didn't misspell any Heart, Target, Challenge, or Alternate Words, mark Lessons 2 and 3 complete and move to the online activity for Day 4 to practice for the Unit Checkpoint on Day 5.

Heart Words

➲ *Skip this activity if students didn't misspell any Heart Words on this unit's pretest.*

1. **Gather** the Words to Learn cards for any Heart Words.

2. **Practice** the *new* Heart Words.

3. **Practice** *all* Heart Words.

4. **Track mastery** of Heart Words.

Target Words

➲ *Skip this activity if students didn't misspell any Target Words on this unit's pretest.*

1. **Gather** the Words to Learn cards for any Target Words.

2. **Discover** the new spelling convention.

3. **Practice** the Target Words.

Challenge Words

> *Skip this activity if students are struggling with the Heart Words and Target Words.*

1. **Gather** the Words to Learn cards for any Challenge Words.
2. **Discover** the new spelling convention in the Challenge Words.
3. **Practice** the Challenge Words.

Alternate Words

> *Skip this activity if students don't have any Words to Learn cards for Alternate Words.*

1. **Gather** the Words to Learn cards for any Alternate Words.
2. **Discover** the new spelling convention in the Alternate Words.
3. **Practice** the Alternate Words.

Day 2 ....

Practice Spelling Words

Practice using the Activity Bank.

Day 3 ....

Practice Spelling Words

Practice using the Activity Bank.

 **15** minutes

Day 4 ....

Review Spelling Words

Review using the online activity.

[Offline] ⏱ 15 minutes

Unit Checkpoint

1. **Dictate** the Words to Learn.

2. **Check** students' answers.

3. **Review** the words students misspelled.

Rewards:

- Help students find and play the online Spelling game, Spell 'n' Stack. Students should use levels 1–3.

- If students scored 80 percent or above on the Unit Checkpoint, add a sticker to the Unit 5 box on students' My Accomplishments chart. If students scored under 80 percent, continue to practice the words that they missed and add a sticker to this unit once they have mastered the words.

Review Heart Words, Short Vowel Sounds, Suffixes –s & –es, –ng & –nk Words, and Long a & i Spellings

In this unit, students will review the spelling conventions and Heart Words they studied in the previous five units. Refer to the Unit Plans of previous units for a detailed description of each spelling convention.

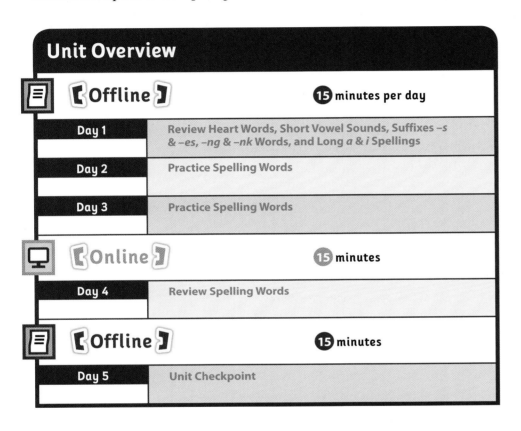

Unit Overview

Offline — 15 minutes per day

Day 1	Review Heart Words, Short Vowel Sounds, Suffixes –s & –es, –ng & –nk Words, and Long a & i Spellings
Day 2	Practice Spelling Words
Day 3	Practice Spelling Words

Online — 15 minutes

| Day 4 | Review Spelling Words |

Offline — 15 minutes

| Day 5 | Unit Checkpoint |

Objectives

- Spell Heart Words.
- Spell words containing short vowel sounds.
- Spell plurals ending in –s or –es.
- Spell words ending in –ang, –ing, –ong, or –ung.
- Spell words ending in –ank, –ink, –onk, or –unk.
- Spell words containing the long a sound spelled a, ai, ay, eigh, or a-consonant-e.
- Spell words containing the long i sound spelled i, ie, igh, y, or i-consonant-e.

Heart Words

have	brown	done
may	cold	her
say	come	keep
hard	once	these
both	does	every
been	do	

Target Words

until	string	lame
happen	yank	silent
objects	always	inside
riches		

Alternate Words

unrest	brink	alight
steps	crate	

Challenge Words

raining	firelight	elegant

[Offline] ⓯ minutes per day

Complete the Spelling activities with students. **For the full instructions for each activity, refer to pages SP 8–13.**

Day 1

Review Heart Words, Short Vowel Sounds, Suffixes –s & –es, –ng & –nk Words, and Long *a* & *i* Spellings

[Materials]

- index cards (8)
- whiteboard (optional)

Advance Preparation

Gather the index cards you made previously for the Heart and Target Words listed. Write each Challenge and Alternate Word on a separate index card. Indicate on each card whether a word is a Challenge or Alternate Word.

Pretest

1. **Administer** a pretest using the Heart and Target Words.

2. **Gather** students' Words to Learn cards.

Note: If students didn't misspell any Heart, Target, Challenge, or Alternate Words, mark Lessons 2 and 3 complete and move to the online activity for Day 4 to practice for the Unit Checkpoint on Day 5.

Heart Words

➲ *Skip this activity if students didn't misspell any Heart Words on this unit's pretest.*

1. **Gather** the Words to Learn cards for any Heart Words.

2. **Practice** the Heart Words.

3. **Track mastery** of Heart Words.

Target Words

➲ *Skip this activity if students didn't misspell any Target Words on this unit's pretest.*

1. **Gather** the Words to Learn cards for any Target Words.

2. **Review** the previously studied spelling convention in each Target Word.

3. **Practice** the Target Words.

Challenge Words

➲ *Skip this activity if students are struggling with the Heart Words and Target Words.*

1. **Gather** the Words to Learn cards for any Challenge Words.
2. **Review** the previously studied spelling convention in each Challenge Word.
3. **Practice** the Challenge Words.

Alternate Words

➲ *Skip this activity if students don't have any Words to Learn cards for Alternate Words.*

1. **Gather** the Words to Learn cards for any Alternate Words.
2. **Review** the previously studied spelling convention in each Alternate Word.
3. **Practice** the Alternate Words.

Day 2 ....

Practice Spelling Words

Practice using the Activity Bank.

Day 3 ....

Practice Spelling Words

Practice using the Activity Bank.

 minutes

Day 4 ....

Review Spelling Words

Review using the online activity.

Offline ⏱ **15** minutes

Day 5

Unit Checkpoint

1. **Dictate** the Words to Learn.

2. **Check** students' answers.

3. **Review** the words students misspelled.

Rewards:

- Help students find and play the online Spelling game, Spell 'n' Stack. Students should use levels 1–3.

- If students scored 80 percent or above on the Unit Checkpoint, add a sticker to the Unit 6 box on students' My Accomplishments chart. If students scored under 80 percent, continue to practice the words that they missed and add a sticker to this unit once they have mastered the words.

Heart Words and Long *o* Spellings

Target spelling convention — **letter combinations that create the long *o* sound**

The most common spellings for the long *o* sound are *o, oa, oe, ow, ough*, and *o-consonant-e*. Each of this unit's Target Words contains the long *o* sound spelled with one of these letter combinations.

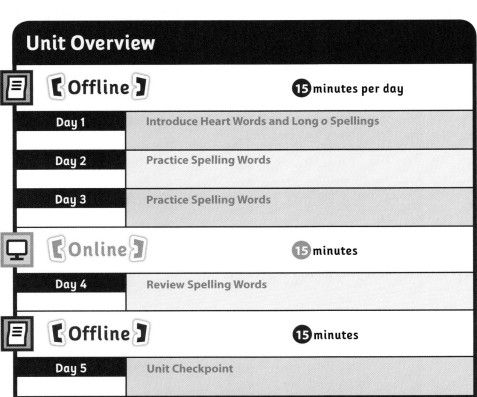

Unit Overview

📋 〔 Offline 〕　　　⏱15 minutes per day

Day 1	Introduce Heart Words and Long *o* Spellings
Day 2	Practice Spelling Words
Day 3	Practice Spelling Words

💻 〔 Online 〕　　　⏱15 minutes

| Day 4 | Review Spelling Words |

📋 〔 Offline 〕　　　⏱15 minutes

| Day 5 | Unit Checkpoint |

☁️ Heart Words

| from | full | found |
| for | | |

⭐ Challenge Words

| alone | although | thorough |
| known | | |

◎ Target Words

dough	woe	shown
locate	volcano	window
float	follow	stone
almost		

Alternate Words

hole	sailboat	throw
tiptoe	though	doe
crossroad	rowboat	roast
bloat		

 **Offline** ⏱ **15 minutes per day**

Complete the Spelling activities with students. **For the full instructions for each activity, refer to pages SP 8–13.**

Day 1

Introduce Heart Words and Long *o* Spellings

 **Materials**

- index cards (28)
- whiteboard (optional)

Advance Preparation

Write each Heart, Target, Challenge, and Alternate Word on a separate index card. Indicate on each card whether a word is a Heart, Target, Challenge, or Alternate Word.

Pretest

1. **Administer** a pretest using the Heart and Target Words.

2. **Gather** students' Words to Learn cards.

Note: If students didn't misspell any Heart, Target, Challenge, or Alternate Words, mark Lessons 2 and 3 complete and move to the online activity for Day 4 to practice for the Unit Checkpoint on Day 5.

Heart Words

➲ *Skip this activity if students didn't misspell any Heart Words on this unit's pretest.*

1. **Gather** the Words to Learn cards for any Heart Words.

2. **Practice** the *new* Heart Words.

3. **Practice** *all* Heart Words.

4. **Track mastery** of Heart Words.

Target Words

➲ *Skip this activity if students didn't misspell any Target Words on this unit's pretest.*

1. **Gather** the Words to Learn cards for any Target Words.

2. **Discover** the new spelling convention.

3. **Practice** the Target Words.

Challenge Words

⮑ *Skip this activity if students are struggling with the Heart Words and Target Words.*

1. **Gather** the Words to Learn cards for any Challenge Words.
2. **Discover** the new spelling convention in the Challenge Words.
3. **Practice** the Challenge Words.

Alternate Words

⮑ *Skip this activity if students don't have any Words to Learn cards for Alternate Words.*

1. **Gather** the Words to Learn cards for any Alternate Words.
2. **Discover** the new spelling convention in the Alternate Words.
3. **Practice** the Alternate Words.

Day 2 ....

Practice Spelling Words

Practice using the Activity Bank.

Day 3 ....

Practice Spelling Words

Practice using the Activity Bank.

 **15 minutes**

Day 4 ....

Review Spelling Words

Review using the online activity.

【 Offline 】 ⑮ minutes

Unit Checkpoint

1. **Dictate** the Words to Learn.

2. **Check** students' answers.

3. **Review** the words students misspelled.

Rewards:

- Help students find and play the online Spelling game, Spell 'n' Stack. Students should use levels 1–3.

- If students scored 80 percent or above on the Unit Checkpoint, add a sticker to the Unit 7 box on students' My Accomplishments chart. If students scored under 80 percent, continue to practice the words that they missed and add a sticker to this unit once they have mastered the words.

Heart Words and Long *e* Spellings

Target spelling convention — **letter combinations that create the long *e* sound**

The most common spellings for the long *e* sound are *e*, *ee*, *ea*, *ie*, *y*, and *e*-consonant-*e*. Each of this unit's Target Words contains the long *e* sound spelled with one of these letter combinations.

Unit Overview

📄 【Offline】 ⏱15 minutes per day

Day 1	Introduce Heart Words and Long *e* Spellings
Day 2	Practice Spelling Words
Day 3	Practice Spelling Words

🖥 【Online】 ⏱15 minutes

| Day 4 | Review Spelling Words |

📄 【Offline】 ⏱15 minutes

| Day 5 | Unit Checkpoint |

♡ Heart Words

| good | laugh | today |

⭐ Challenge Words

| between | probably | represent |
| company | | |

◎ Target Words

street	complete	quickly
details	leave	yield
even	real	least
athlete		

Alternate Words

teaching	chief	between
steel	seem	agreed
easy	field	melody
body		

[Offline] 🕐 minutes per day

Complete the Spelling activities with students. **For the full instructions for each activity, refer to pages SP 8–13.**

Day 1

Introduce Heart Words and Long e Spellings

[Materials]

- index cards (27)
- whiteboard (optional)

Advance Preparation

Write each Heart, Target, Challenge, and Alternate Word on a separate index card. Indicate on each card whether a word is a Heart, Target, Challenge, or Alternate Word.

Pretest

1. **Administer** a pretest using the Heart and Target Words.

2. **Gather** students' Words to Learn cards.

Note: If students didn't misspell any Heart, Target, Challenge, or Alternate Words, mark Lessons 2 and 3 complete and move to the online activity for Day 4 to practice for the Unit Checkpoint on Day 5.

Heart Words

⮑ *Skip this activity if students didn't misspell any Heart Words on this unit's pretest.*

1. **Gather** the Words to Learn cards for any Heart Words.

2. **Practice** the *new* Heart Words.

3. **Practice** *all* Heart Words.

4. **Track mastery** of Heart Words.

Target Words

⮑ *Skip this activity if students didn't misspell any Target Words on this unit's pretest.*

1. **Gather** the Words to Learn cards for any Target Words.

2. **Discover** the new spelling convention.

3. **Practice** the Target Words.

Challenge Words

↪ *Skip this activity if students are struggling with the Heart Words and Target Words.*

1. **Gather** the Words to Learn cards for any Challenge Words.
2. **Discover** the new spelling convention in the Challenge Words.
3. **Practice** the Challenge Words.

Alternate Words

↪ *Skip this activity if students don't have any Words to Learn cards for Alternate Words.*

1. **Gather** the Words to Learn cards for any Alternate Words.
2. **Discover** the new spelling convention in the Alternate Words.
3. **Practice** the Alternate Words.

Day 2

Practice Spelling Words

Practice using the Activity Bank.

Day 3

Practice Spelling Words

Practice using the Activity Bank.

 **15** minutes

Day 4

Review Spelling Words

Review using the online activity.

 **15** minutes

Day 5

Unit Checkpoint

1. **Dictate** the Words to Learn.

2. **Check** students' answers.

3. **Review** the words students misspelled.

 Rewards:

- Help students find and play the online Spelling game, Spell 'n' Stack. Students should use levels 1–3.

- If students scored 80 percent or above on the Unit Checkpoint, add a sticker to the Unit 8 box on students' My Accomplishments chart. If students scored under 80 percent, continue to practice the words that they missed and add a sticker to this unit once they have mastered the words.

Heart Words and Long *u* Spellings

Target spelling convention — letter combinations that create the long *u* sound

The most common spellings for the long *u* sound are *u*, *ue*, *ew*, and *u*-consonant-*e*. Each of this unit's Target Words contains the long *u* sound spelled with one of these letter combinations.

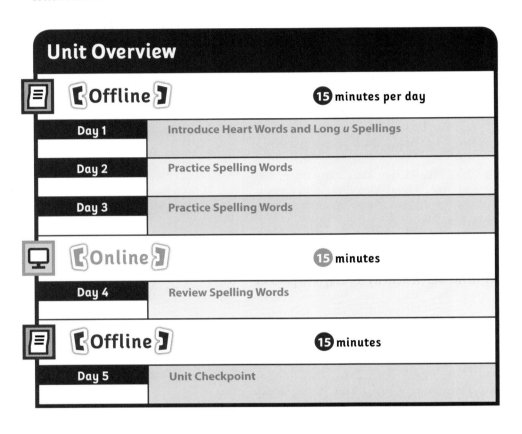

> ### Objectives
> - Spell Heart Words.
> - Spell words containing the long *u* sound spelled *ue*, *ew*, *u*, or *u*-consonant-*e*.

Unit Overview

📄 〔Offline〕 ⏱ 15 minutes per day

Day 1	Introduce Heart Words and Long *u* Spellings
Day 2	Practice Spelling Words
Day 3	Practice Spelling Words

🖥 〔Online〕 ⏱ 15 minutes

Day 4	Review Spelling Words

📄 〔Offline〕 ⏱ 15 minutes

Day 5	Unit Checkpoint

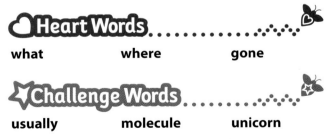

♡ Heart Words

what	where	gone

☆ Challenge Words

usually	molecule	unicorn

◎ Target Words

pew	united	mute
music	museum	cute
bugle	rescue	fumes
curfew		

Alternate Words

humor	value	mew
nephew	unit	continue
refuse	blueprint	utensil
pupil		

[Offline] 🕐 minutes per day

Complete the Spelling activities with students. **For the full instructions for each activity, refer to pages SP 8–13.**

Day 1 ....

Introduce Heart Words and Long *u* Spellings

[Materials]

- index cards (26)
- whiteboard (optional)

Advance Preparation

Write each Heart, Target, Challenge, and Alternate Word on a separate index card. Indicate on each card whether a word is a Heart, Target, Challenge, or Alternate Word.

Pretest

1. **Administer** a pretest using the Heart and Target Words.
2. **Gather** students' Words to Learn cards.

Note: If students didn't misspell any Heart, Target, Challenge, or Alternate Words, mark Lessons 2 and 3 complete and move to the online activity for Day 4 to practice for the Unit Checkpoint on Day 5.

Heart Words

⮑ *Skip this activity if students didn't misspell any Heart Words on this unit's pretest.*

1. **Gather** the Words to Learn cards for any Heart Words.
2. **Practice** the *new* Heart Words.
3. **Practice** *all* Heart Words.
4. **Track mastery** of Heart Words.

Target Words

⮑ *Skip this activity if students didn't misspell any Target Words on this unit's pretest.*

1. **Gather** the Words to Learn cards for any Target Words.
2. **Discover** the new spelling convention.
3. **Practice** the Target Words.

Challenge Words

⮌ *Skip this activity if students are struggling with the Heart Words and Target Words.*

1. **Gather** the Words to Learn cards for any Challenge Words.
2. **Discover** the new spelling convention in the Challenge Words.
3. **Practice** the Challenge Words.

Alternate Words

⮌ *Skip this activity if students don't have any Words to Learn cards for Alternate Words.*

1. **Gather** the Words to Learn cards for any Alternate Words.
2. **Discover** the new spelling convention in the Alternate Words.
3. **Practice** the Alternate Words.

Day 2 ....

Practice Spelling Words

Practice using the Activity Bank.

Day 3 ....

Practice Spelling Words

Practice using the Activity Bank.

 15 minutes

Day 4 ....

Review Spelling Words

Review using the online activity.

[Offline] ⑮ minutes

Day 5

Unit Checkpoint

1. **Dictate** the Words to Learn.

2. **Check** students' answers.

3. **Review** the words students misspelled.

Rewards:

- Help students find and play the online Spelling game, Spell 'n' Stack. Students should use levels 1–3.

- If students scored 80 percent or above on the Unit Checkpoint, add a sticker to the Unit 9 box on students' My Accomplishments chart. If students scored under 80 percent, continue to practice the words that they missed and add a sticker to this unit once they have mastered the words.

Heart Words and Long Double *o* Spellings

Target spelling convention — **letter combinations that create the long double *o* sound**

The most common spellings for the long double *o* sound are *oo, u, ue, ew, ou,* and *u*-consonant-*e*. Each of this unit's Target Words contains the long double *o* sound spelled with one of these letter combinations.

★ **Objectives**
- Spell Heart Words.
- Spell words containing the long double *o* sound spelled *oo, u, ue, ew, ou,* and *u*-consonant-*e*.

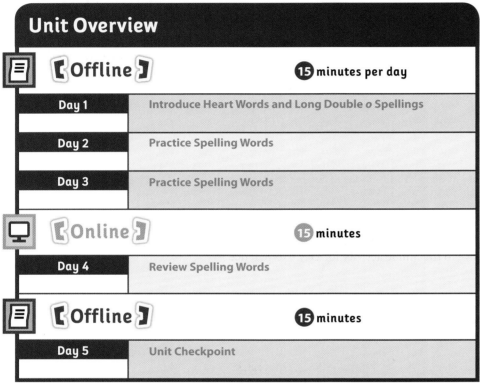

Unit Overview

📋 【 Offline 】   ⑮ minutes per day

Day 1	Introduce Heart Words and Long Double *o* Spellings
Day 2	Practice Spelling Words
Day 3	Practice Spelling Words

🖥 【 Online 】   ⑮ minutes

Day 4	Review Spelling Words

📋 【 Offline 】   ⑮ minutes

Day 5	Unit Checkpoint

♡ Heart Words

is	into	again

☆ Challenge Words

smooth	toothpaste	shampoo

◎ Target Words

ruby	soup	spoon
rule	student	true
include	July	bamboo
grew		

Alternate Words

tune	flew	usual
snoop	hoot	cool
loose	group	renew
fool		

[Offline] ⏱ 15 minutes per day

Complete the Spelling activities with students. **For the full instructions for each activity, refer to pages SP 8–13.**

 Day 1 ....

Introduce Heart Words and Long Double *o* Spellings

Materials

- index cards (26)
- whiteboard (optional)

Advance Preparation

Write each Heart, Target, Challenge, and Alternate Word on a separate index card. Indicate on each card whether a word is a Heart, Target, Challenge, or Alternate Word.

Pretest

1. **Administer** a pretest using the Heart and Target Words.

2. **Gather** students' Words to Learn cards.

Note: If students didn't misspell any Heart, Target, Challenge, or Alternate Words, mark Lessons 2 and 3 complete and move to the online activity for Day 4 to practice for the Unit Checkpoint on Day 5.

Heart Words

⮑ *Skip this activity if students didn't misspell any Heart Words on this unit's pretest.*

1. **Gather** the Words to Learn cards for any Heart Words.

2. **Practice** the *new* Heart Words.

3. **Practice** *all* Heart Words.

4. **Track mastery** of Heart Words.

Target Words

⮑ *Skip this activity if students didn't misspell any Target Words on this unit's pretest.*

1. **Gather** the Words to Learn cards for any Target Words.

2. **Discover** the new spelling convention.

3. **Practice** the Target Words.

Challenge Words

↪ *Skip this activity if students are struggling with the Heart Words and Target Words.*

1. **Gather** the Words to Learn cards for any Challenge Words.
2. **Discover** the new spelling convention in the Challenge Words.
3. **Practice** the Challenge Words.

Alternate Words

↪ *Skip this activity if students don't have any Words to Learn cards for Alternate Words.*

1. **Gather** the Words to Learn cards for any Alternate Words.
2. **Discover** the new spelling convention in the Alternate Words.
3. **Practice** the Alternate Words.

Day 2 ···

Practice Spelling Words

Practice using the Activity Bank.

Day 3 ···

Practice Spelling Words

Practice using the Activity Bank.

 **15 minutes**

Day 4 ···

Review Spelling Words

Review using the online activity.

【 Offline 】 ⏱ 15 minutes

Unit Checkpoint

1. **Dictate** the Words to Learn.

2. **Check** students' answers.

3. **Review** the words students misspelled.

Rewards:

- Help students find and play the online Spelling game, Spell 'n' Stack. Students should use levels 1–3.

- If students scored 80 percent or above on the Unit Checkpoint, add a sticker to the Unit 10 box on students' My Accomplishments chart. If students scored under 80 percent, continue to practice the words that they missed and add a sticker to this unit once they have mastered the words.

Heart Words and /ow/ & /oi/ Spellings

Target spelling convention — **letter combinations that create the /ow/ and /oi/ sounds**

The sound /ow/ can be spelled *ou* or *ow*. The sound /oi/ can be spelled *oi* or *oy*. Each of this unit's Target Words contains the sound /ow/ or the sound /oi/.

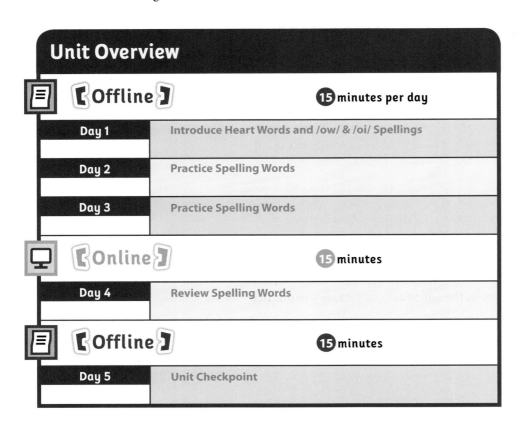

Unit Overview

Offline — 15 minutes per day

Day 1	Introduce Heart Words and /ow/ & /oi/ Spellings
Day 2	Practice Spelling Words
Day 3	Practice Spelling Words

Online — 15 minutes

| Day 4 | Review Spelling Words |

Offline — 15 minutes

| Day 5 | Unit Checkpoint |

Heart Words

could   would   should

Challenge Words

around   about   thousands
mountain

Target Words

count	toil	enjoy
south	soil	destroy
ground	joint	flowers
sound		

Alternate Words

crown	cloudy	recoil
vowel	pounds	downtown
point	outline	amount
loyal		

[Offline] 🕒 minutes per day

Complete the Spelling activities with students. **For the full instructions for each activity, refer to pages SP 8–13.**

Day 1

Introduce Heart Words and /ow/ & /oi/ Spellings

Materials
- index cards (27)
- whiteboard (optional)

Advance Preparation

Write each Heart, Target, Challenge, and Alternate Word on a separate index card. Indicate on each card whether a word is a Heart, Target, Challenge, or Alternate Word.

Pretest

1. **Administer** a pretest using the Heart and Target Words.

2. **Gather** students' Words to Learn cards.

Note: If students didn't misspell any Heart, Target, Challenge, or Alternate Words, mark Lessons 2 and 3 complete and move to the online activity for Day 4 to practice for the Unit Checkpoint on Day 5.

Heart Words

➲ *Skip this activity if students didn't misspell any Heart Words on this unit's pretest.*

1. **Gather** the Words to Learn cards for any Heart Words.

2. **Practice** the *new* Heart Words.

3. **Practice** *all* Heart Words.

4. **Track mastery** of Heart Words.

Target Words

➲ *Skip this activity if students didn't misspell any Target Words on this unit's pretest.*

1. **Gather** the Words to Learn cards for any Target Words.

2. **Discover** the new spelling convention.

3. **Practice** the Target Words.

Challenge Words

➲ *Skip this activity if students are struggling with the Heart Words and Target Words.*

1. **Gather** the Words to Learn cards for any Challenge Words.
2. **Discover** the new spelling convention in the Challenge Words.
3. **Practice** the Challenge Words.

Alternate Words

➲ *Skip this activity if students don't have any Words to Learn cards for Alternate Words.*

1. **Gather** the Words to Learn cards for any Alternate Words.
2. **Discover** the new spelling convention in the Alternate Words.
3. **Practice** the Alternate Words.

Day 2 ....

Practice Spelling Words

Practice using the Activity Bank.

Day 3 ....

Practice Spelling Words

Practice using the Activity Bank.

 **15 minutes**

Day 4 ....

Review Spelling Words

Review using the online activity.

[Offline] 🕘 **minutes**

Unit Checkpoint

1. **Dictate** the Words to Learn.

2. **Check** students' answers.

3. **Review** the words students misspelled.

Rewards:

- Help students find and play the online Spelling game, Spell 'n' Stack. Students should use levels 1–3.

- If students scored 80 percent or above on the Unit Checkpoint, add a sticker to the Unit 11 box on students' My Accomplishments chart. If students scored under 80 percent, continue to practice the words that they missed and add a sticker to this unit once they have mastered the words.

Review Heart Words; Long *o*, *e*, & *u* Spellings; Long Double *o* Spellings; and /ow/ & /oi/ Spellings

In this unit, students will review the spelling conventions and Heart Words they studied in the previous five units. Refer to the Unit Plans of previous units for a detailed description of each spelling convention.

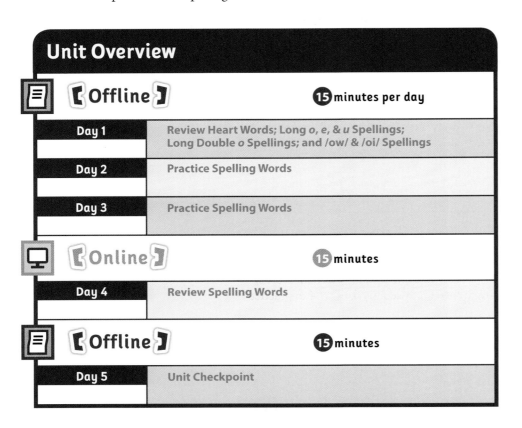

Unit Overview

Offline — 15 minutes per day

Day 1	Review Heart Words; Long *o*, *e*, & *u* Spellings; Long Double *o* Spellings; and /ow/ & /oi/ Spellings
Day 2	Practice Spelling Words
Day 3	Practice Spelling Words

Online — 15 minutes

| Day 4 | Review Spelling Words |

Offline — 15 minutes

| Day 5 | Unit Checkpoint |

Objectives

- Spell Heart Words.
- Spell words containing the long *o* sound spelled *o*, *oa*, *oe*, *ow*, *ough*, or *o-consonant-e*.
- Spell words containing the long *e* sound spelled *e*, *ee*, *ea*, *ie*, *y*, and *e-consonant-e*.
- Spell words containing the long *u* sound spelled *ue*, *ew*, *u*, or *u-consonant-e*.
- Spell words containing the long double *o* sound spelled *oo*, *u*, *ue*, *ew*, *ou*, and *u-consonant-e*.
- Spell words containing the sound /ow/ spelled *ou* or *ow*.
- Spell words containing the sound /oi/ spelled *oi* or *oy*.

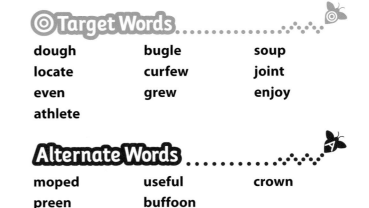

Heart Words

from	today	into
for	what	again
full	where	could
found	gone	would
good	is	should
laugh		

Challenge Words

review	rowboat	uncoil

Target Words

dough	bugle	soup
locate	curfew	joint
even	grew	enjoy
athlete		

Alternate Words

moped	useful	crown
preen	buffoon	

Offline **15** minutes per day

Complete the Spelling activities with students. **For the full instructions for each activity, refer to pages SP 8–13.**

Day 1 ....

Review Heart Words; Long *o*, *e*, & *u* Spellings; Long Double *o* Spellings; and /ow/ & /oi/ Spellings

Materials

- index cards (8)
- whiteboard (optional)

Advance Preparation

Gather the index cards you made previously for the Heart and Target Words listed. Write each Challenge and Alternate Word on a separate index card. Indicate on each card whether a word is a Challenge or Alternate Word.

Pretest

1. **Administer** a pretest using the Heart and Target Words.
2. **Gather** students' Words to Learn cards.

Note: If students didn't misspell any Heart, Target, Challenge, or Alternate Words, mark Lessons 2 and 3 complete and move to the online activity for Day 4 to practice for the Unit Checkpoint on Day 5.

Heart Words

➲ *Skip this activity if students didn't misspell any Heart Words on this unit's pretest.*

1. **Gather** the Words to Learn cards for any Heart Words.
2. **Practice** the Heart Words.
3. **Track mastery** of Heart Words.

Target Words

➲ *Skip this activity if students didn't misspell any Target Words on this unit's pretest.*

1. **Gather** the Words to Learn cards for any Target Words.
2. **Review** the previously studied spelling convention in each Target Word.
3. **Practice** the Target Words.

Challenge Words

➲ *Skip this activity if students are struggling with the Heart Words and Target Words.*

1. **Gather** the Words to Learn cards for any Challenge Words.
2. **Review** the previously studied spelling convention in each Challenge Word.
3. **Practice** the Challenge Words.

Alternate Words

➲ *Skip this activity if students don't have any Words to Learn cards for Alternate Words.*

1. **Gather** the Words to Learn cards for any Alternate Words.
2. **Review** the previously studied spelling convention in each Alternate Word.
3. **Practice** the Alternate Words.

Day 2 ···

Practice Spelling Words

Practice using the Activity Bank.

Day 3 ···

Practice Spelling Words

Practice using the Activity Bank.

 **15** minutes

Day 4 ···

Review Spelling Words

Review using the online activity.

【 Offline 】 ⏱ minutes

Unit Checkpoint

1. **Dictate** the Words to Learn.

2. **Check** students' answers.

3. **Review** the words students misspelled.

Rewards:

- Help students find and play the online Spelling game, Spell 'n' Stack. Students should use levels 1–3.

- If students scored 80 percent or above on the Unit Checkpoint, add a sticker to the Unit 12 box on students' My Accomplishments chart. If students scored under 80 percent, continue to practice the words that they missed and add a sticker to this unit once they have mastered the words.

Heart Words and /ur/ Spellings

Target spelling convention — **letter combinations that create the /ur/ sound**

The most common spellings for the sound /ur/ are *er*, *ir*, *ur*, and *ear*. Each of this unit's Target Words contains the sound /ur/ spelled with one of these letter combinations.

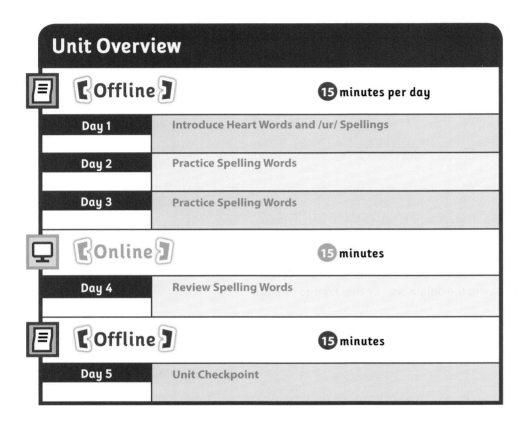

Unit Overview

📋 〔Offline〕 ⏱15 minutes per day

Day 1	Introduce Heart Words and /ur/ Spellings
Day 2	Practice Spelling Words
Day 3	Practice Spelling Words

🖥 〔Online〕 ⏱15 minutes

Day 4	Review Spelling Words

📋 〔Offline〕 ⏱15 minutes

Day 5	Unit Checkpoint

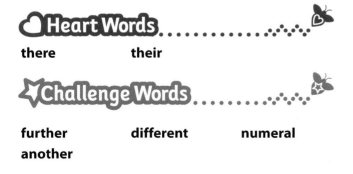

☁ Heart Words

there   their

★ Challenge Words

further   different   numeral

another

◎ Target Words

earth	lurk	eastern
learn	northern	third
earn	southern	girl
curd		

Alternate Words

rather	ever	early
together	hurt	pattern
strummer	never	birth
return		

 **Offline** ⏱ **15** minutes per day

Complete the Spelling activities with students. **For the full instructions for each activity, refer to pages SP 8–13.**

Introduce Heart Words and /ur/ Spellings

 **Materials**

- index cards (26)
- whiteboard (optional)

Advance Preparation

Write each Heart, Target, Challenge, and Alternate Word on a separate index card. Indicate on each card whether a word is a Heart, Target, Challenge, or Alternate Word.

Pretest

1. **Administer** a pretest using the Heart and Target Words.

2. **Gather** students' Words to Learn cards.

Note: If students didn't misspell any Heart, Target, Challenge, or Alternate Words, mark Lessons 2 and 3 complete and move to the online activity for Day 4 to practice for the Unit Checkpoint on Day 5.

Heart Words

➲ *Skip this activity if students didn't misspell any Heart Words on this unit's pretest.*

1. **Gather** the Words to Learn cards for any Heart Words.

2. **Practice** the *new* Heart Words.

3. **Practice** *all* Heart Words.

4. **Track mastery** of Heart Words.

Target Words

➲ *Skip this activity if students didn't misspell any Target Words on this unit's pretest.*

1. **Gather** the Words to Learn cards for any Target Words.

2. **Discover** the new spelling convention.

3. **Practice** the Target Words.

Challenge Words

⮑ *Skip this activity if students are struggling with the Heart Words and Target Words.*

1. **Gather** the Words to Learn cards for any Challenge Words.
2. **Discover** the new spelling convention in the Challenge Words.
3. **Practice** the Challenge Words.

Alternate Words

⮑ *Skip this activity if students don't have any Words to Learn cards for Alternate Words.*

1. **Gather** the Words to Learn cards for any Alternate Words.
2. **Discover** the new spelling convention in the Alternate Words.
3. **Practice** the Alternate Words.

Day 2 ·

Practice Spelling Words

Practice using the Activity Bank.

Day 3 ·

Practice Spelling Words

Practice using the Activity Bank.

 **15 minutes**

Day 4 ·

Review Spelling Words

Review using the online activity.

〔 Offline 〕 15 minutes

Unit Checkpoint

1. **Dictate** the Words to Learn.
2. **Check** students' answers.
3. **Review** the words students misspelled.

Rewards:

- Help students find and play the online Spelling game, Spell 'n' Stack. Students should use levels 1–3.

- If students scored 80 percent or above on the Unit Checkpoint, add a sticker to the Unit 13 box on students' My Accomplishments chart. If students scored under 80 percent, continue to practice the words that they missed and add a sticker to this unit once they have mastered the words.

Heart Words and Long *e* & Long *i* Spelled *y*

Target spelling convention — **using *y* to create a long *e* or a long *i* sound**

When it appears at the end of a syllable, the letter *y* can have either the long *e* sound or the long *i* sound. Each of this unit's Target Words contains a syllable ending in *y*.

Objectives
- Spell Heart Words.
- Spell words containing the long *e* or long *i* sounds spelled with the letter *y*.

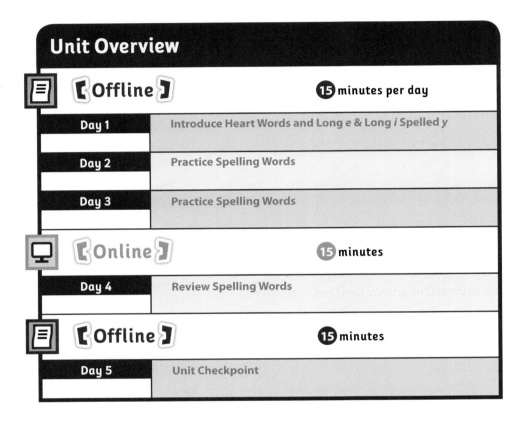

Unit Overview

[Offline] 15 minutes per day

Day 1	Introduce Heart Words and Long *e* & Long *i* Spelled *y*
Day 2	Practice Spelling Words
Day 3	Practice Spelling Words

[Online] 15 minutes

Day 4	Review Spelling Words

[Offline] 15 minutes

Day 5	Unit Checkpoint

Heart Words

many	story	country

Challenge Words

noisy	qualify	multiply
crybaby		

Target Words

penny	fluffy	notify
sturdy	copy	apply
hurry	pry	deny
fuzzy		

Alternate Words

defy	spy	study
empty	family	windy
reply	amplify	lumpy
hungry		

[Offline] ⑮ minutes per day

Complete the Spelling activities with students. **For the full instructions for each activity, refer to pages SP 8–13.**

....

Introduce Heart Words and Long *e* & Long *i* Spelled *y*

[Materials]

- index cards (27)
- whiteboard (optional)

Advance Preparation

Write each Heart, Target, Challenge, and Alternate Word on a separate index card. Indicate on each card whether a word is a Heart, Target, Challenge, or Alternate Word.

Pretest

1. **Administer** a pretest using the Heart and Target Words.

2. **Gather** students' Words to Learn cards.

Note: If students didn't misspell any Heart, Target, Challenge, or Alternate Words, mark Lessons 2 and 3 complete and move to the online activity for Day 4 to practice for the Unit Checkpoint on Day 5.

Heart Words

➲ *Skip this activity if students didn't misspell any Heart Words on this unit's pretest.*

1. **Gather** the Words to Learn cards for any Heart Words.

2. **Practice** the *new* Heart Words.

3. **Practice** *all* Heart Words.

4. **Track mastery** of Heart Words.

Target Words

➲ *Skip this activity if students didn't misspell any Target Words on this unit's pretest.*

1. **Gather** the Words to Learn cards for any Target Words.

2. **Discover** the new spelling convention.

3. **Practice** the Target Words.

Challenge Words

➲ *Skip this activity if students are struggling with the Heart Words and Target Words.*

1. **Gather** the Words to Learn cards for any Challenge Words.
2. **Discover** the new spelling convention in the Challenge Words.
3. **Practice** the Challenge Words.

Alternate Words

➲ *Skip this activity if students don't have any Words to Learn cards for Alternate Words.*

1. **Gather** the Words to Learn cards for any Alternate Words.
2. **Discover** the new spelling convention in the Alternate Words.
3. **Practice** the Alternate Words.

Day 2

Practice Spelling Words

Practice using the Activity Bank.

Day 3

Practice Spelling Words

Practice using the Activity Bank.

 **minutes**

Day 4

Review Spelling Words

Review using the online activity.

[Offline] ⏱ 15 minutes

Unit Checkpoint

1. **Dictate** the Words to Learn.

2. **Check** students' answers.

3. **Review** the words students misspelled.

Rewards:

- Help students find and play the online Spelling game, Spell 'n' Stack. Students should use levels 1–3.

- If students scored 80 percent or above on the Unit Checkpoint, add a sticker to the Unit 14 box on students' My Accomplishments chart. If students scored under 80 percent, continue to practice the words that they missed and add a sticker to this unit once they have mastered the words.

Heart Words and Vowel Suffixes on Words Ending in *y*

Target spelling convention — **words ending in *y* + vowel suffixes**

A vowel suffix is a suffix that begins with a vowel. Base words that end in *y* do not change when the vowel suffix *–ing* is added. However, when the vowel suffixes *–ed*, *–er*, and *–es* are added to base words that end in *y*, change the *y* to *i* before adding the suffix. Each of this unit's Target Words ends in the vowel suffix *–ing*, *–ed*, *–er*, or *–es*.

Objectives
- Spell Heart Words.
- Spell words ending with the vowel suffixes *–ing*, *–ed*, *–er*, or *–es*.

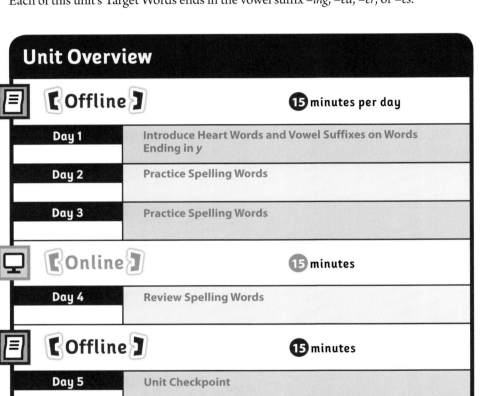

Unit Overview		
〔Offline〕		**15** minutes per day
Day 1	Introduce Heart Words and Vowel Suffixes on Words Ending in *y*	
Day 2	Practice Spelling Words	
Day 3	Practice Spelling Words	
〔Online〕		**15** minutes
Day 4	Review Spelling Words	
〔Offline〕		**15** minutes
Day 5	Unit Checkpoint	

Heart Words

minute   build   very

Challenge Words

carries   marries   marrying
carried

Target Words

flies	burying	hurried
spies	studying	cried
prettier	ladies	happier
trying		

Alternate Words

berries	stickier	carrying
ponies	bunnies	crazier
grouchier	easier	lying
replies		

【 Offline 】 ⑮ minutes per day

Complete the Spelling activities with students. **For the full instructions for each activity, refer to pages SP 8–13.**

....

Introduce Heart Words and Vowel Suffixes on Words Ending in *y*

【 **Materials** 】

- index cards (27)
- whiteboard (optional)

Advance Preparation

Write each Heart, Target, Challenge, and Alternate Word on a separate index card. Indicate on each card whether a word is a Heart, Target, Challenge, or Alternate Word.

Pretest

1. **Administer** a pretest using the Heart and Target Words.

2. **Gather** students' Words to Learn cards.

Note: If students didn't misspell any Heart, Target, Challenge, or Alternate Words, mark Lessons 2 and 3 complete and move to the online activity for Day 4 to practice for the Unit Checkpoint on Day 5.

Heart Words

⮑ *Skip this activity if students didn't misspell any Heart Words on this unit's pretest.*

1. **Gather** the Words to Learn cards for any Heart Words.

2. **Practice** the *new* Heart Words.

3. **Practice** *all* Heart Words.

4. **Track mastery** of Heart Words.

Target Words

⮑ *Skip this activity if students didn't misspell any Target Words on this unit's pretest.*

1. **Gather** the Words to Learn cards for any Target Words.

2. **Discover** the new spelling convention.

3. **Practice** the Target Words.

Challenge Words

➲ *Skip this activity if students are struggling with the Heart Words and Target Words.*

1. **Gather** the Words to Learn cards for any Challenge Words.
2. **Discover** the new spelling convention in the Challenge Words.
3. **Practice** the Challenge Words.

Alternate Words

➲ *Skip this activity if students don't have any Words to Learn cards for Alternate Words.*

1. **Gather** the Words to Learn cards for any Alternate Words.
2. **Discover** the new spelling convention in the Alternate Words.
3. **Practice** the Alternate Words.

Day 2 ....

Practice Spelling Words

Practice using the Activity Bank.

Day 3 ....

Practice Spelling Words

Practice using the Activity Bank.

 **15 minutes**

Day 4 ....

Review Spelling Words

Review using the online activity.

[Offline] ⏱ 15 minutes

Day 5

Unit Checkpoint

1. **Dictate** the Words to Learn.

2. **Check** students' answers.

3. **Review** the words students misspelled.

Rewards:

- Help students find and play the online Spelling game, Spell 'n' Stack. Students should use levels 1–3.

- If students scored 80 percent or above on the Unit Checkpoint, add a sticker to the Unit 15 box on students' My Accomplishments chart. If students scored under 80 percent, continue to practice the words that they missed and add a sticker to this unit once they have mastered the words.

Heart Words and Dropping Silent *e* Before Vowel Suffixes

Target spelling convention — base word ending in a silent *e* + vowel suffix *–ed*, *–er*, or *–ing*

When adding a vowel suffix to a base word that ends with a silent *e*, drop the *e* before adding the vowel suffix. Each of this unit's Target Words is a word ending in a silent *e* that has had the vowel suffix *–ed*, *–er*, or *–ing* added.

Objectives

- Spell Heart Words.
- Spell words requiring the silent *e* to be dropped before adding a vowel suffix.

Unit Overview

▤ 〖 Offline 〗   15 minutes per day

Day 1	Introduce Heart Words and Dropping Silent *e* Before Vowel Suffixes
Day 2	Practice Spelling Words
Day 3	Practice Spelling Words

🖥 〖 Online 〗   15 minutes

Day 4	Review Spelling Words

▤ 〖 Offline 〗   15 minutes

Day 5	Unit Checkpoint

☁ Heart Words

please	woman	give

★ Challenge Words

moving	mover	replaced

◎ Target Words

graded	using	wasting
grading	user	smiled
grader	wasted	smiling
used		

Alternate Words

hoped	dined	baking
liking	baker	liked
hoping	dining	diner
baked		

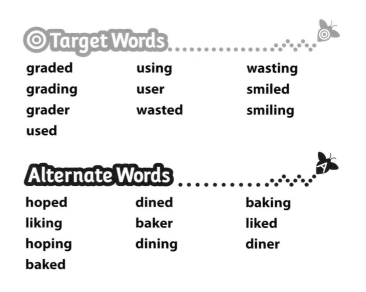

[Offline] ⏱ 15 minutes per day

Complete the Spelling activities with students. **For the full instructions for each activity, refer to pages SP 8–13.**

Day 1

Introduce Heart Words and Dropping Silent *e* Before Vowel Suffixes

[Materials]

- index cards (26)
- whiteboard (optional)

Advance Preparation

Write each Heart, Target, Challenge, and Alternate Word on a separate index card. Indicate on each card whether a word is a Heart, Target, Challenge, or Alternate Word.

Pretest

1. **Administer** a pretest using the Heart and Target Words.
2. **Gather** students' Words to Learn cards.

Note: If students didn't misspell any Heart, Target, Challenge, or Alternate Words, mark Lessons 2 and 3 complete and move to the online activity for Day 4 to practice for the Unit Checkpoint on Day 5.

Heart Words

⊃ *Skip this activity if students didn't misspell any Heart Words on this unit's pretest.*

1. **Gather** the Words to Learn cards for any Heart Words.
2. **Practice** the *new* Heart Words.
3. **Practice** *all* Heart Words.
4. **Track mastery** of Heart Words.

Target Words

⊃ *Skip this activity if students didn't misspell any Target Words on this unit's pretest.*

1. **Gather** the Words to Learn cards for any Target Words.
2. **Discover** the new spelling convention.
3. **Practice** the Target Words.

Challenge Words

↪ *Skip this activity if students are struggling with the Heart Words and Target Words.*

1. **Gather** the Words to Learn cards for any Challenge Words.
2. **Discover** the new spelling convention in the Challenge Words.
3. **Practice** the Challenge Words.

Alternate Words

↪ *Skip this activity if students don't have any Words to Learn cards for Alternate Words.*

1. **Gather** the Words to Learn cards for any Alternate Words.
2. **Discover** the new spelling convention in the Alternate Words.
3. **Practice** the Alternate Words.

Day 2 ....

Practice Spelling Words

Practice using the Activity Bank.

Day 3 ....

Practice Spelling Words

Practice using the Activity Bank.

 **15 minutes**

Day 4 ....

Review Spelling Words

Review using the online activity.

[Offline] ⏱ 15 minutes

Unit Checkpoint

1. **Dictate** the Words to Learn.

2. **Check** students' answers.

3. **Review** the words students misspelled.

Rewards:

- Help students find and play the online Spelling game, Spell 'n' Stack. Students should use levels 1–3.

- If students scored 80 percent or above on the Unit Checkpoint, add a sticker to the Unit 16 box on students' My Accomplishments chart. If students scored under 80 percent, continue to practice the words that they missed and add a sticker to this unit once they have mastered the words.

Heart Words and Doubling Consonants Before Adding Vowel Suffixes

Target spelling convention — doubled final consonants + vowel suffixes

When adding a vowel suffix to a one-syllable base word that ends with one vowel followed by a consonant, double the consonant before adding the vowel suffix. Each of this unit's Target Words is a one-syllable base word ending with one vowel followed by a consonant that has been doubled before adding the vowel suffix.

Unit Overview

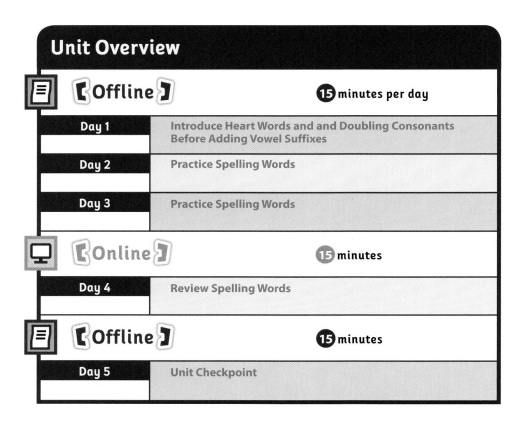

	Offline	**15** minutes per day
Day 1	Introduce Heart Words and and Doubling Consonants Before Adding Vowel Suffixes	
Day 2	Practice Spelling Words	
Day 3	Practice Spelling Words	

	Online	**15** minutes
Day 4	Review Spelling Words	

	Offline	**15** minutes
Day 5	Unit Checkpoint	

Heart Words

north   warm

Challenge Words

beginning   omitted   kidnapper

Target Words

runner	stopped	topping
trapper	flipped	plopped
dotted	spotter	stepped
potting		

Alternate Words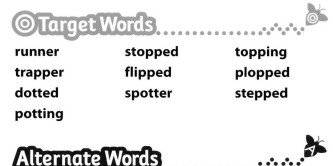

clapped	quitting	batted
thinner	whipping	planner
mopping	setter	fitted
mapping		

[Offline] 🕘 minutes per day

Complete the Spelling activities with students. **For the full instructions for each activity, refer to pages SP 8–13.**

Introduce Heart Words and Doubling Consonants Before Adding Vowel Suffixes

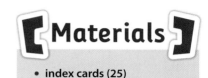

[Materials]

- index cards (25)
- whiteboard (optional)

Advance Preparation

Write each Heart, Target, Challenge, and Alternate Word on a separate index card. Indicate on each card whether a word is a Heart, Target, Challenge, or Alternate Word.

Pretest

1. **Administer** a pretest using the Heart and Target Words.

2. **Gather** students' Words to Learn cards.

Note: If students didn't misspell any Heart, Target, Challenge, or Alternate Words, mark Lessons 2 and 3 complete and move to the online activity for Day 4 to practice for the Unit Checkpoint on Day 5.

Heart Words

⮑ *Skip this activity if students didn't misspell any Heart Words on this unit's pretest.*

1. **Gather** the Words to Learn cards for any Heart Words.

2. **Practice** the *new* Heart Words.

3. **Practice** *all* Heart Words.

4. **Track mastery** of Heart Words.

Target Words

⮑ *Skip this activity if students didn't misspell any Target Words on this unit's pretest.*

1. **Gather** the Words to Learn cards for any Target Words.

2. **Discover** the new spelling convention.

3. **Practice** the Target Words.

Challenge Words

⮑ *Skip this activity if students are struggling with the Heart Words and Target Words.*

1. **Gather** the Words to Learn cards for any Challenge Words.
2. **Discover** the new spelling convention in the Challenge Words.
3. **Practice** the Challenge Words.

Alternate Words

⮑ *Skip this activity if students don't have any Words to Learn cards for Alternate Words.*

1. **Gather** the Words to Learn cards for any Alternate Words.
2. **Discover** the new spelling convention in the Alternate Words.
3. **Practice** the Alternate Words.

Day 2 ....

Practice Spelling Words

Practice using the Activity Bank.

Day 3 ....

Practice Spelling Words

Practice using the Activity Bank.

 **15 minutes**

Day 4 ....

Review Spelling Words

Review using the online activity.

[Offline] ⓯ minutes

Day 5

Unit Checkpoint

1. **Dictate** the Words to Learn.

2. **Check** students' answers.

3. **Review** the words students misspelled.

Rewards:

- Help students find and play the online Spelling game, Spell 'n' Stack. Students should use levels 1–3.

- If students scored 80 percent or above on the Unit Checkpoint, add a sticker to the Unit 17 box on students' My Accomplishments chart. If students scored under 80 percent, continue to practice the words that they missed and add a sticker to this unit once they have mastered the words.

Review Heart Words, /ur/ Spellings, Long *e* & *i* Spelled *y*, and Adding Vowel Suffixes

In this unit, students will review the spelling conventions and Heart Words they studied in the previous five units. Refer to the Unit Plans of previous units for a detailed description of each spelling convention.

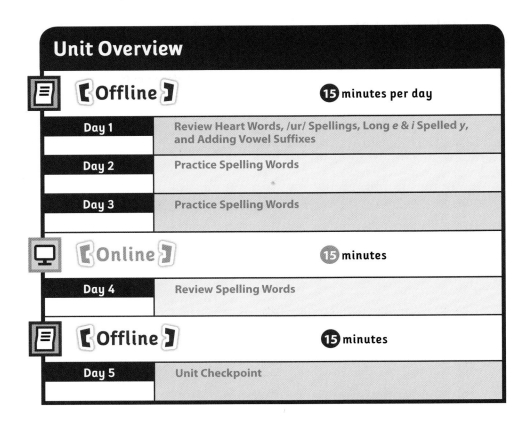

Unit Overview

Offline — 15 minutes per day

Day 1	Review Heart Words, /ur/ Spellings, Long *e* & *i* Spelled *y*, and Adding Vowel Suffixes
Day 2	Practice Spelling Words
Day 3	Practice Spelling Words

Online — 15 minutes

| Day 4 | Review Spelling Words |

Offline — 15 minutes

| Day 5 | Unit Checkpoint |

Objectives
- Spell Heart Words.
- Spell words containing the sound /ur/ spelled *er*, *ir*, *ur*, and *ear*.
- Spell words containing the long *e* or long *i* sounds spelled with the letter *y*.
- Spell words ending with the vowel suffixes –*ing*, –*ed*, –*er*, or –*es*.
- Spell words requiring the silent *e* to be dropped before adding a vowel suffix.
- Spell words requiring doubling the final consonant before adding a vowel suffix.

Heart Words

there	please	north
their	woman	warm
many	give	minute
story	very	build
country		

Target Words

earth	flies	smiling
southern	studying	runner
penny	wasted	stepped
notify		

Challenge Words

| equipped | funeral | resuming |

Alternate Words

| revert | messier | skipped |
| trusty | blaming | |

[Offline] 🕐 minutes per day

Complete the Spelling activities with students. **For the full instructions for each activity, refer to pages SP 8–13.**

Day 1

Review Heart Words, /ur/ Spellings, Long *e* & *i* Spelled *y*, and Adding Vowel Suffixes

Materials

- index cards (8)
- whiteboard (optional)

Advance Preparation

Gather the index cards you made previously for the Heart and Target Words listed. Write each Challenge and Alternate Word on a separate index card. Indicate on each card whether a word is a Challenge or Alternate Word.

Pretest

1. **Administer** a pretest using the Heart and Target Words.
2. **Gather** students' Words to Learn cards.

Note: If students didn't misspell any Heart, Target, Challenge, or Alternate Words, mark Lessons 2 and 3 complete and move to the online activity for Day 4 to practice for the Unit Checkpoint on Day 5.

Heart Words

⮑ *Skip this activity if students didn't misspell any Heart Words on this unit's pretest.*

1. **Gather** the Words to Learn cards for any Heart Words.
2. **Practice** the Heart Words.
3. **Track mastery** of Heart Words.

Target Words

⮑ *Skip this activity if students didn't misspell any Target Words on this unit's pretest.*

1. **Gather** the cards for any Target Words.
2. **Review** the previously studied spelling convention in each Target Word.
3. **Practice** the Target Words.

Challenge Words

⮑ *Skip this activity if students are struggling with the Heart Words and Target Words.*

1. **Gather** the Words to Learn cards for any Challenge Words.
2. **Review** the previously studied spelling convention in each Challenge Word.
3. **Practice** the Challenge Words.

Alternate Words

⮑ *Skip this activity if students don't have any Words to Learn cards for Alternate Words.*

1. **Gather** the Words to Learn cards for any Alternate Words.
2. **Review** the previously studied spelling convention in each Alternate Word.
3. **Practice** the Alternate Words.

Day 2 ....

Practice Spelling Words

Practice using the Activity Bank.

Day 3 ....

Practice Spelling Words

Practice using the Activity Bank.

 ⓯ minutes

Day 4 ....

Review Spelling Words

Review using the online activity.

[Offline] ⓯ minutes

Unit Checkpoint

1. **Dictate** the Words to Learn.

2. **Check** students' answers.

3. **Review** the words students misspelled.

Rewards:

- Help students find and play the online Spelling game, Spell 'n' Stack. Students should use levels 1–3.

- If students scored 80 percent or above on the Unit Checkpoint, add a sticker to the Unit 18 box on students' My Accomplishments chart. If students scored under 80 percent, continue to practice the words that they missed and add a sticker to this unit once they have mastered the words.

Heart Words and Soft *c* & *g* Spellings

Target spelling convention — **creating the /s/ sound with the letter *c* and the /j/ sound with the letter *g***

The letter *c* almost always has the sound /s/ when it is followed by *e, i,* or *y.* Sometimes the letter *g* has the sound /j/ when it is followed by *e, i,* or *y.* However, there are many exceptions to this convention. Each of this unit's Target Words contains the sound /s/ spelled *c* or the sound /j/ spelled *g.*

Objectives
- Spell Heart Words.
- Spell words containing the sound /s/ spelled *c.*
- Spell words containing the sound /j/ spelled *g.*

Unit Overview

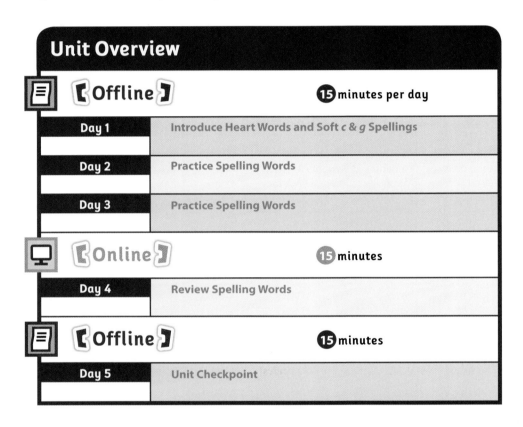

📄 **Offline**	🕐 15 minutes per day
Day 1	Introduce Heart Words and Soft *c* & *g* Spellings
Day 2	Practice Spelling Words
Day 3	Practice Spelling Words

🖥 **Online**	🕐 15 minutes
Day 4	Review Spelling Words

📄 **Offline**	🕐 15 minutes
Day 5	Unit Checkpoint

☁ Heart Words

eye	cousin

⭐ Challenge Words

oxygen	piece	surface
sincere		

◎ Target Words

decimal	voice	huge
sentence	general	strange
center	gelatin	change
nice		

Alternate Words

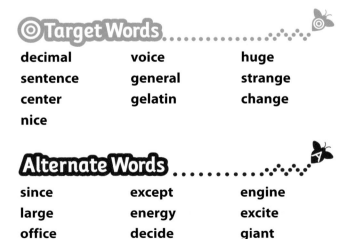

since	except	engine
large	energy	excite
office	decide	giant
stage		

[Offline] ⏱ **15** minutes per day

Complete the Spelling activities with students. **For the full instructions for each activity, refer to pages SP 8–13.**

Day 1 ....

Introduce Heart Words and Soft *c* & *g* Spellings

[**Materials**]

- index cards (26)
- whiteboard (optional)

Advance Preparation

Write each Heart, Target, Challenge, and Alternate Word on a separate index card. Indicate on each card whether a word is a Heart, Target, Challenge, or Alternate Word.

Pretest

1. **Administer** a pretest using the Heart and Target Words.

2. **Gather** students' Words to Learn cards.

Note: If students didn't misspell any Heart, Target, Challenge, or Alternate Words, mark Lessons 2 and 3 complete and move to the online activity for Day 4 to practice for the Unit Checkpoint on Day 5.

Heart Words

➦ *Skip this activity if students didn't misspell any Heart Words on this unit's pretest.*

1. **Gather** the Words to Learn cards for any Heart Words.

2. **Practice** the *new* Heart Words.

3. **Practice** *all* Heart Words.

4. **Track mastery** of Heart Words.

Target Words

➦ *Skip this activity if students didn't misspell any Target Words on this unit's pretest.*

1. **Gather** the Words to Learn cards for any Target Words.

2. **Discover** the new spelling convention.

3. **Practice** the Target Words.

Challenge Words

➲ *Skip this activity if students are struggling with the Heart Words and Target Words.*

1. **Gather** the Words to Learn cards for any Challenge Words.
2. **Discover** the new spelling convention in the Challenge Words.
3. **Practice** the Challenge Words.

Alternate Words

➲ *Skip this activity if students don't have any Words to Learn cards for Alternate Words.*

1. **Gather** the Words to Learn cards for any Alternate Words.
2. **Discover** the new spelling convention in the Alternate Words.
3. **Practice** the Alternate Words.

Day 2 ....

Practice Spelling Words

Practice using the Activity Bank.

Day 3 ....

Practice Spelling Words

Practice using the Activity Bank.

 **15 minutes**

Day 4 ....

Review Spelling Words

Review using the online activity.

 **Offline** ⏱ **15** minutes

Unit Checkpoint

1. **Dictate** the Words to Learn.

2. **Check** students' answers.

3. **Review** the words students misspelled.

Rewards:

- Help students find and play the online Spelling game, Spell 'n' Stack. Students should use levels 1–3.

- If students scored 80 percent or above on the Unit Checkpoint, add a sticker to the Unit 19 box on students' My Accomplishments chart. If students scored under 80 percent, continue to practice the words that they missed and add a sticker to this unit once they have mastered the words.

Heart Words and /aw/ & /z/ Spellings

Target spelling convention – **using *al* to create the /aw/ sound; using *ze* or *se* to create the /z/ sound**

The sound /aw/ can be spelled with the letters *al*. Two common spellings of the sound /z/ at the end of a word are *ze* and *se*. Each of this unit's Target Words contains the sound /aw/ spelled *al* or the sound /z/ spelled *ze* or *se*.

Objectives
- Spell Heart Words.
- Spell words containing the sound /aw/ spelled *al*.
- Spell words containing the sound /z/ spelled *ze* and *se*.

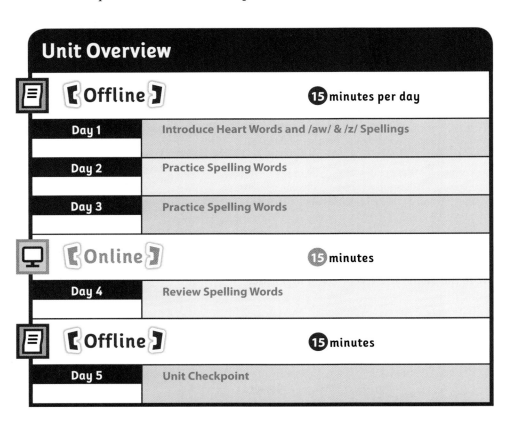

Unit Overview

📄	**❪Offline❫**	**🕐15 minutes per day**
Day 1	Introduce Heart Words and /aw/ & /z/ Spellings	
Day 2	Practice Spelling Words	
Day 3	Practice Spelling Words	

💻	**❪Online❫**	**🕐15 minutes**
Day 4	Review Spelling Words	

📄	**❪Offline❫**	**🕐15 minutes**
Day 5	Unit Checkpoint	

♡ Heart Words

dozen	season	lose

☆ Challenge Words

balk	laser	trapeze
prison		

◎ Target Words

talk	suppose	rosebush
stalk	sneeze	those
bald	cheese	chose
hose		

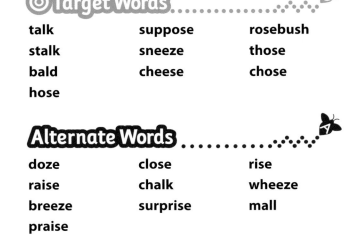

Alternate Words

doze	close	rise
raise	chalk	wheeze
breeze	surprise	mall
praise		

 **Offline** **15 minutes per day**

Complete the Spelling activities with students. **For the full instructions for each activity, refer to pages SP 8–13.**

Day 1

Introduce Heart Words and /aw/ & /z/ Spellings

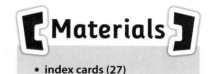

Materials

- index cards (27)
- whiteboard (optional)

Advance Preparation

Write each Heart, Target, Challenge, and Alternate Word on a separate index card. Indicate on each card whether a word is a Heart, Target, Challenge, or Alternate Word.

Pretest

1. **Administer** a pretest using the Heart and Target Words.
2. **Gather** students' Words to Learn cards.

Note: If students didn't misspell any Heart, Target, Challenge, or Alternate Words, mark Lessons 2 and 3 complete and move to the online activity for Day 4 to practice for the Unit Checkpoint on Day 5.

Heart Words

➲ *Skip this activity if students didn't misspell any Heart Words on this unit's pretest.*

1. **Gather** the Words to Learn cards for any Heart Words.
2. **Practice** the *new* Heart Words.
3. **Practice** *all* Heart Words.
4. **Track mastery** of Heart Words.

Target Words

➲ *Skip this activity if students didn't misspell any Target Words on this unit's pretest.*

1. **Gather** the Words to Learn cards for any Target Words.
2. **Discover** the new spelling convention.
3. **Practice** the Target Words.

Challenge Words

⮩ *Skip this activity if students are struggling with the Heart Words and Target Words.*

1. **Gather** the Words to Learn cards for any Challenge Words.
2. **Discover** the new spelling convention in the Challenge Words.
3. **Practice** the Challenge Words.

Alternate Words

⮩ *Skip this activity if students don't have any Words to Learn cards for Alternate Words.*

1. **Gather** the Words to Learn cards for any Alternate Words.
2. **Discover** the new spelling convention in the Alternate Words.
3. **Practice** the Alternate Words.

Day 2 ....

Practice Spelling Words

Practice using the Activity Bank.

Day 3 ....

Practice Spelling Words

Practice using the Activity Bank.

 15 minutes

Day 4 ....

Review Spelling Words

Review using the online activity.

[Offline] 🕧 minutes

Day 5

Unit Checkpoint

1. **Dictate** the Words to Learn.

2. **Check** students' answers.

3. **Review** the words students misspelled.

Rewards:

- Help students find and play the online Spelling game, Spell 'n' Stack. Students should use levels 1–3.

- If students scored 80 percent or above on the Unit Checkpoint, add a sticker to the Unit 20 box on students' My Accomplishments chart. If students scored under 80 percent, continue to practice the words that they missed and add a sticker to this unit once they have mastered the words.

Heart Words and Triple Consonant Blends

Target spelling convention — **common triple consonant blends**

A triple consonant blend is a blend in which the sounds of three consonants in a row can be heard. Common triple consonant blends include *scr*, *spr*, *spl*, and *str*. The letters *squ* are a triple consonant blend in which the *u* represents the /w/ sound. Each of this unit's Target Words contains a triple consonant blend.

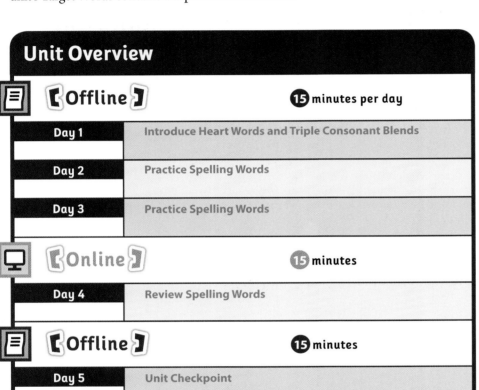

Unit Overview

📋 **[Offline]**   ⏱ **15** minutes per day

Day 1	Introduce Heart Words and Triple Consonant Blends
Day 2	Practice Spelling Words
Day 3	Practice Spelling Words

🖥 **[Online]**   ⏱ **15** minutes

| Day 4 | Review Spelling Words |

📋 **[Offline]**   ⏱ **15** minutes

| Day 5 | Unit Checkpoint |

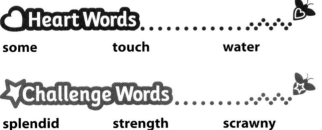

☁ Heart Words

some	touch	water

★ Challenge Words

splendid	strength	scrawny

© Target Words

script	splash	strap
scrap	split	squash
spring	stress	square
spray		

Alternate Words

sprain	straw	screw
squeeze	splice	squint
spread	stream	scrape
splat		

[Offline] ⑮ minutes per day

Complete the Spelling activities with students. **For the full instructions for each activity, refer to pages SP 8–13.**

For the full instructions for each activity, refer to pages SP 8–13.

Day 1

Introduce Heart Words and Triple Consonant Blends

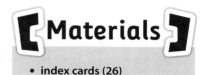

[Materials]

- index cards (26)
- whiteboard (optional)

Advance Preparation

Write each Heart, Target, Challenge, and Alternate Word on a separate index card. Indicate on each card whether a word is a Heart, Target, Challenge, or Alternate Word.

Pretest

1. **Administer** a pretest using the Heart and Target Words.

2. **Gather** students' Words to Learn cards.

Note: If students didn't misspell any Heart, Target, Challenge, or Alternate Words, mark Lessons 2 and 3 complete and move to the online activity for Day 4 to practice for the Unit Checkpoint on Day 5.

Heart Words

➲ *Skip this activity if students didn't misspell any Heart Words on this unit's pretest.*

1. **Gather** the Words to Learn cards for any Heart Words.

2. **Practice** the *new* Heart Words.

3. **Practice** *all* Heart Words.

4. **Track mastery** of Heart Words.

Target Words

➲ *Skip this activity if students didn't misspell any Target Words on this unit's pretest.*

1. **Gather** the Words to Learn cards for any Target Words.

2. **Discover** the new spelling convention.

3. **Practice** the Target Words.

Challenge Words

➲ *Skip this activity if students are struggling with the Heart Words and Target Words.*

1. **Gather** the Words to Learn cards for any Challenge Words.
2. **Discover** the new spelling convention in the Challenge Words.
3. **Practice** the Challenge Words.

Alternate Words

➲ *Skip this activity if students don't have any Words to Learn cards for Alternate Words.*

1. **Gather** the Words to Learn cards for any Alternate Words.
2. **Discover** the new spelling convention in the Alternate Words.
3. **Practice** the Alternate Words.

Day 2 ....

Practice Spelling Words

Practice using the Activity Bank.

Day 3 ....

Practice Spelling Words

Practice using the Activity Bank.

 **15 minutes**

Day 4 ....

Review Spelling Words

Review using the online activity.

[Offline] ⏱ **15** minutes

Day 5

Unit Checkpoint

1. **Dictate** the Words to Learn.

2. **Check** students' answers.

3. **Review** the words students misspelled.

Rewards:

- Help students find and play the online Spelling game, Spell 'n' Stack. Students should use levels 1–3.

- If students scored 80 percent or above on the Unit Checkpoint, add a sticker to the Unit 21 box on students' My Accomplishments chart. If students scored under 80 percent, continue to practice the words that they missed and add a sticker to this unit once they have mastered the words.

Heart Words, Digraphs, and Trigraphs

Target spelling convention — words containing the digraphs *sh*, *th*, *ch* and *ph*; words containing the trigraphs *dge* and *tch*

Two letters that spell only one sound are called a digraph. Some common digraphs are *sh*, *th*, *ch*, and *ph*. Three letters that spell only one sound are called a trigraph. The letters *dge* are a trigraph representing the sound /j/, and the letters *tch* are a trigraph representing the sound /ch/. Each of this unit's Target Words contains either a digraph or a trigraph.

Objectives
- Spell Heart Words.
- Spell words containing the digraphs *sh*, *th*, *ch*, and *ph*.
- Spell words containing the trigraphs *dge* and *tch*.

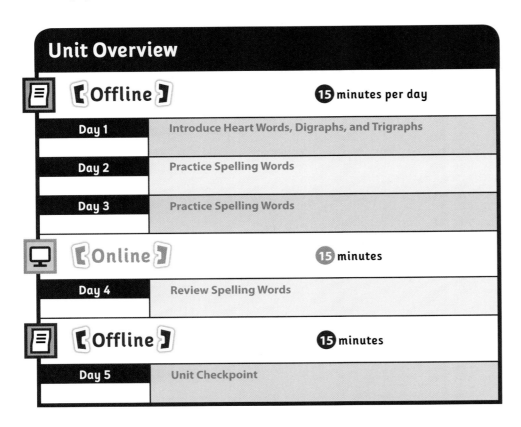

Unit Overview

	Offline	🕐 **15 minutes per day**
Day 1	Introduce Heart Words, Digraphs, and Trigraphs	
Day 2	Practice Spelling Words	
Day 3	Practice Spelling Words	

	Online	🕐 **15 minutes**
Day 4	Review Spelling Words	

	Offline	🕐 **15 minutes**
Day 5	Unit Checkpoint	

Heart Words
mother   brother   father

Challenge Words
catcher   paragraph   telephone

Target Words
shrimp	phonics	badge
threw	phrase	match
branch	edge	catch
bunch		

Alternate Words
throne	ridge	fudge
kitchen	hedge	thrill
lunch	shrink	stitch
pitcher		

 **Offline** ⏱ **15** minutes per day

Complete the Spelling activities with students. **For the full instructions for each activity, refer to pages SP 8–13.**

Day 1

Introduce Heart Words, Digraphs, and Trigraphs

 **Materials**
- index cards (26)
- whiteboard (optional)

Advance Preparation

Write each Heart, Target, Challenge, and Alternate Word on a separate index card. Indicate on each card whether a word is a Heart, Target, Challenge, or Alternate Word.

Pretest

1. **Administer** a pretest using the Heart and Target Words.
2. **Gather** students' Words to Learn cards.

Note: If students didn't misspell any Heart, Target, Challenge, or Alternate Words, mark Lessons 2 and 3 complete and move to the online activity for Day 4 to practice for the Unit Checkpoint on Day 5.

Heart Words

⮌ *Skip this activity if students didn't misspell any Heart Words on this unit's pretest.*

1. **Gather** the Words to Learn cards for any Heart Words.
2. **Practice** the *new* Heart Words.
3. **Practice** *all* Heart Words.
4. **Track mastery** of Heart Words.

Target Words

⮌ *Skip this activity if students didn't misspell any Target Words on this unit's pretest.*

1. **Gather** the Words to Learn cards for any Target Words.
2. **Discover** the new spelling convention.
3. **Practice** the Target Words.

Challenge Words

⮑ *Skip this activity if students are struggling with the Heart Words and Target Words.*

1. **Gather** the Words to Learn cards for any Challenge Words.
2. **Discover** the new spelling convention in the Challenge Words.
3. **Practice** the Challenge Words.

Alternate Words

⮑ *Skip this activity if students don't have any Words to Learn cards for Alternate Words.*

1. **Gather** the Words to Learn cards for any Alternate Words.
2. **Discover** the new spelling convention in the Alternate Words.
3. **Practice** the Alternate Words.

Day 2 ....

Practice Spelling Words

Practice using the Activity Bank.

Day 3 ....

Practice Spelling Words

Practice using the Activity Bank.

 **15** minutes

Day 4 ....

Review Spelling Words

Review using the online activity.

〔Offline〕 ⑮ minutes

Day 5

Unit Checkpoint

1. **Dictate** the Words to Learn.

2. **Check** students' answers.

3. **Review** the words students misspelled.

Rewards:

- Help students find and play the online Spelling game, Spell 'n' Stack. Students should use levels 1–3.

- If students scored 80 percent or above on the Unit Checkpoint, add a sticker to the Unit 22 box on students' My Accomplishments chart. If students scored under 80 percent, continue to practice the words that they missed and add a sticker to this unit once they have mastered the words.

Heart Words, Contractions, and Consonant Suffixes

Target spelling convention — **using contractions to condense two words into one; adding a consonant suffix to a base word**

A contraction is one word made from two. An apostrophe represents the dropped letters. A consonant suffix begins with a consonant, and adding the suffix does not change the base word's spelling. Each of the Target Words in this unit is a contraction or has a consonant suffix.

Objectives
- Spell Heart Words.
- Spell contractions.
- Spell words ending with consonant suffixes.

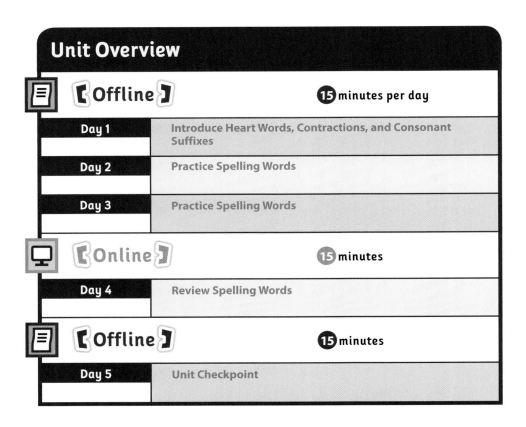

Unit Overview

⊟	**〘 Offline 〙**	**⑮ minutes per day**
Day 1	Introduce Heart Words, Contractions, and Consonant Suffixes	
Day 2	Practice Spelling Words	
Day 3	Practice Spelling Words	
💻	**〘 Online 〙**	**⑮ minutes**
Day 4	Review Spelling Words	
⊟	**〘 Offline 〙**	**⑮ minutes**
Day 5	Unit Checkpoint	

♡ Heart Words

world   were

★ Challenge Words

thoughtless   commitment   arrangement

◎ Target Words

I'm	careless	punishment
he's	useless	shipment
isn't	aimless	basement
can't		

Alternate Words

priceless	she's	lawful
tireless	doesn't	agreement
fearless	it's	wishful
shouldn't		

 Offline ⏱ **15 minutes per day**

Complete the Spelling activities with students. **For the full instructions for each activity, refer to pages SP 8–13.**

Day 1

Introduce Heart Words, Contractions, and Consonant Suffixes

Materials

- index cards (25)
- whiteboard (optional)

Advance Preparation

Write each Heart, Target, Challenge, and Alternate Word on a separate index card. Indicate on each card whether a word is a Heart, Target, Challenge, or Alternate Word.

Pretest

1. **Administer** a pretest using the Heart and Target Words.
2. **Gather** students' Words to Learn cards.

Note: If students didn't misspell any Heart, Target, Challenge, or Alternate Words, mark Lessons 2 and 3 complete and move to the online activity for Day 4 to practice for the Unit Checkpoint on Day 5.

Heart Words

➲ *Skip this activity if students didn't misspell any Heart Words on this unit's pretest.*

1. **Gather** the Words to Learn cards for any Heart Words.
2. **Practice** the *new* Heart Words.
3. **Practice** *all* Heart Words.
4. **Track mastery** of Heart Words.

Target Words

➲ *Skip this activity if students didn't misspell any Target Words on this unit's pretest.*

1. **Gather** the Words to Learn cards for any Target Words.
2. **Discover** the new spelling convention.
3. **Practice** the Target Words.

Challenge Words

➲ *Skip this activity if students are struggling with the Heart Words and Target Words.*

1. **Gather** the Words to Learn cards for any Challenge Words.
2. **Discover** the new spelling convention in the Challenge Words.
3. **Practice** the Challenge Words.

Alternate Words

➲ *Skip this activity if students don't have any Words to Learn cards for Alternate Words.*

1. **Gather** the Words to Learn cards for any Alternate Words.
2. **Discover** the new spelling convention in the Alternate Words.
3. **Practice** the Alternate Words.

Day 2 ....

Practice Spelling Words

Practice using the Activity Bank.

Day 3 ....

Practice Spelling Words

Practice using the Activity Bank.

 **15 minutes**

Day 4 ....

Review Spelling Words

Review using the online activity.

〔 Offline 〕 ⏱ 15 minutes

Day 5

Unit Checkpoint

1. **Dictate** the Words to Learn.

2. **Check** students' answers.

3. **Review** the words students misspelled.

Rewards:

- Help students find and play the online Spelling game, Spell 'n' Stack. Students should use levels 1–3.

- If students scored 80 percent or above on the Unit Checkpoint, add a sticker to the Unit 23 box on students' My Accomplishments chart. If students scored under 80 percent, continue to practice the words that they missed and add a sticker to this unit once they have mastered the words.

Review Heart Words, Soft *c* & *g*, /aw/ & /z/, Triple Consonant Blends, Digraphs, Trigraphs, Contractions, and Consonant Suffixes

In this unit, students will review the spelling conventions and Heart Words they studied in the previous five units. Refer to the Unit Plans of previous units for a detailed description of each spelling convention.

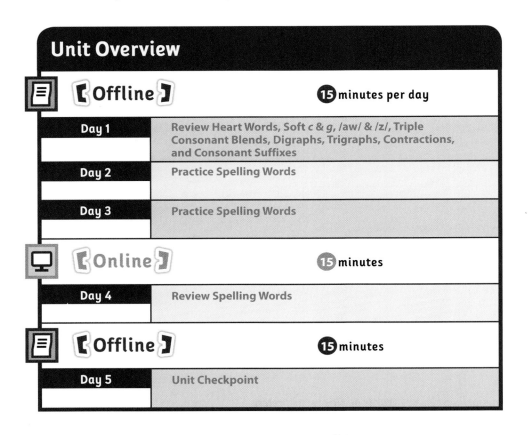

Unit Overview

Offline — 15 minutes per day

Day 1	Review Heart Words, Soft *c* & *g*, /aw/ & /z/, Triple Consonant Blends, Digraphs, Trigraphs, Contractions, and Consonant Suffixes
Day 2	Practice Spelling Words
Day 3	Practice Spelling Words

Online — 15 minutes

Day 4	Review Spelling Words

Offline — 15 minutes

Day 5	Unit Checkpoint

Heart Words

eye	some	brother
cousin	touch	father
dozen	water	world
season	mother	were
lose		

Target Words

decimal	spring	badge
general	squash	he's
talk	threw	useless
cheese		

Challenge Words

pesticide	vengeful	concealment

Alternate Words

splurge	squid	artful
choose	hitch	

[Offline] ⏱ 15 minutes per day

Complete the Spelling activities with students. **For the full instructions for each activity, refer to pages SP 8–13.**

Day 1 ....

Review Heart Words, Soft *c* & *g*, /aw/ & /z/, Triple Consonant Blends, Digraphs, Trigraphs, Contractions, and Consonant Suffixes

[Materials]

- index cards (8)
- whiteboard (optional)

Advance Preparation

Gather the index cards you made previously for the Heart and Target Words listed. Write each Challenge and Alternate Word on a separate index card. Indicate on each card whether a word is a Challenge or Alternate Word.

Pretest

1. **Administer** a pretest using the Heart and Target Words.

2. **Gather** students' Words to Learn cards.

Note: If students didn't misspell any Heart, Target, Challenge, or Alternate Words, mark Lessons 2 and 3 complete and move to the online activity for Day 4 to practice for the Unit Checkpoint on Day 5.

Heart Words

➲ *Skip this activity if students didn't misspell any Heart Words on this unit's pretest.*

1. **Gather** the Words to Learn cards for any Heart Words.

2. **Practice** the Heart Words.

3. **Track mastery** of Heart Words.

Target Words

➲ *Skip this activity if students didn't misspell any Target Words on this unit's pretest.*

1. **Gather** the Words to Learn cards for any Target Words.

2. **Review** the previously studied spelling convention in each Target Word.

3. **Practice** the Target Words.

Challenge Words

⮐ *Skip this activity if students are struggling with the Heart Words and Target Words.*

1. **Gather** the Words to Learn cards for any Challenge Words.
2. **Review** the previously studied spelling convention in each Challenge Word.
3. **Practice** the Challenge Words.

Alternate Words

⮐ *Skip this activity if students don't have any Words to Learn cards for Alternate Words.*

1. **Gather** the Words to Learn cards for any Alternate Words.
2. **Review** the previously studied spelling convention in each Alternate Word.
3. **Practice** the Alternate Words.

Day 2 ....

Practice Spelling Words

Practice using the Activity Bank.

Day 3 ....

Practice Spelling Words

Practice using the Activity Bank.

 ⓯ **minutes**

Day 4 ....

Review Spelling Words

Review using the online activity.

[Offline] ⏱ 15 minutes

Unit Checkpoint

1. **Dictate** the Words to Learn.

2. **Check** students' answers.

3. **Review** the words students misspelled.

Rewards:

- Help students find and play the online Spelling game, Spell 'n' Stack. Students should use levels 1–3.

- If students scored 80 percent or above on the Unit Checkpoint, add a sticker to the Unit 24 box on students' My Accomplishments chart. If students scored under 80 percent, continue to practice the words that they missed and add a sticker to this unit once they have mastered the words.

Heart Words and Consonant Suffixes

Target spelling convention — base word + consonant suffix

A consonant suffix is a suffix that begins with a consonant. When a consonant suffix is added to a word, the spelling of the base word does not change. Each of the Target Words in this unit ends with a consonant suffix.

Objectives
- Spell Heart Words.
- Spell words ending with consonant suffixes.

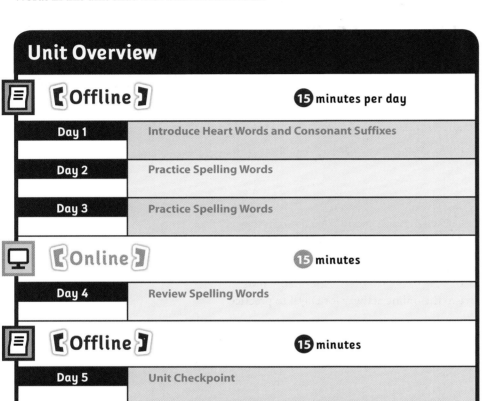

Unit Overview

[Offline]   15 minutes per day

Day 1	Introduce Heart Words and Consonant Suffixes
Day 2	Practice Spelling Words
Day 3	Practice Spelling Words

[Online]   15 minutes

| Day 4 | Review Spelling Words |

[Offline]   15 minutes

| Day 5 | Unit Checkpoint |

Heart Words

love   glove   olive

Challenge Words

cheerfully   carefulness   hopelessly

Target Words

suddenly	kindness	faithful
finally	darkness	peaceful
quickly	strangely	delightful
dampness		

Alternate Words

joyful	careful	blackness
bravely	sickness	totally
hopeful	lonely	crispness
fairness		

[Offline] 🕘 minutes per day

Complete the Spelling activities with students. **For the full instructions for each activity, refer to pages SP 8–13.**

Day 1

Introduce Heart Words and Consonant Suffixes

[Materials]

- index cards (26)
- whiteboard (optional)

Advance Preparation

Write each Heart, Target, Challenge, and Alternate Word on a separate index card. Indicate on each card whether a word is a Heart, Target, Challenge, or Alternate Word.

Pretest

1. **Administer** a pretest using the Heart and Target Words.

2. **Gather** students' Words to Learn cards.

Note: If students didn't misspell any Heart, Target, Challenge, or Alternate Words, mark Lessons 2 and 3 Complete and move to the online activity for Day 4 to practice for the Unit Checkpoint on Day 5.

Heart Words

➲ *Skip this activity if students didn't misspell any Heart Words on this unit's pretest.*

1. **Gather** the Words to Learn cards for any Heart Words.

2. **Practice** the *new* Heart Words.

3. **Practice** *all* Heart Words.

4. **Track mastery** of Heart Words.

Target Words

➲ *Skip this activity if students didn't misspell any Target Words on this unit's pretest.*

1. **Gather** the Words to Learn cards for any Target Words.

2. **Discover** the new spelling convention.

3. **Practice** the Target Words.

Challenge Words

⮑ *Skip this activity if students are struggling with the Heart Words and Target Words.*

1. **Gather** the Words to Learn cards for any Challenge Words.
2. **Discover** the new spelling convention in the Challenge Words.
3. **Practice** the Challenge Words.

Alternate Words

⮑ *Skip this activity if students don't have any Words to Learn cards for Alternate Words.*

1. **Gather** the Words to Learn cards for any Alternate Words.
2. **Discover** the new spelling convention in the Alternate Words.
3. **Practice** the Alternate Words.

Day 2 ....

Practice Spelling Words

Practice using the Activity Bank.

Day 3 ....

Practice Spelling Words

Practice using the Activity Bank.

 **15 minutes**

Day 4 ....

Review Spelling Words

Review using the online activity.

[Offline] **15** minutes

Day 5

Unit Checkpoint

1. **Dictate** the Words to Learn.

2. **Check** students' answers.

3. **Review** the words students misspelled.

Rewards:

- Help students find and play the online Spelling game, Spell 'n' Stack. Students should use levels 1–3.

- If students scored 80 percent or above on the Unit Checkpoint, add a sticker to the Unit 25 box on students' My Accomplishments chart. If students scored under 80 percent, continue to practice the words that they missed and add a sticker to this unit once they have mastered the words.

Heart Words and Prefixes

Target spelling convention — **the prefix *re–*, *dis–*, or *un–* + base word**

When a prefix is added to a base word, the spelling of the base word does not change. Each of the Target Words in this unit begins with the prefix *re–*, *dis–*, or *un–*.

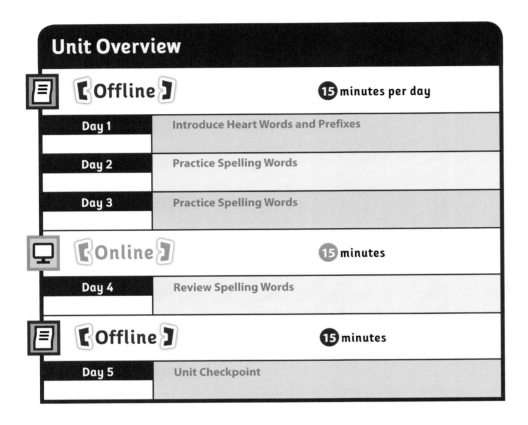

Unit Overview

	Offline	**15** minutes per day
Day 1	Introduce Heart Words and Prefixes	
Day 2	Practice Spelling Words	
Day 3	Practice Spelling Words	

	Online	**15** minutes
Day 4	Review Spelling Words	

	Offline	**15** minutes
Day 5	Unit Checkpoint	

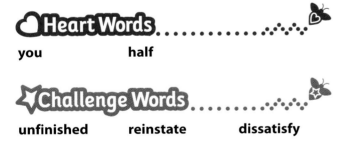

Heart Words

you   half

Challenge Words

unfinished   reinstate   dissatisfy

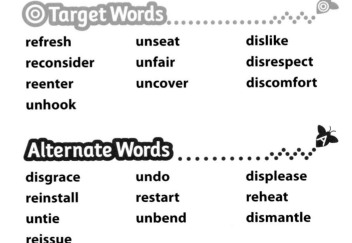

Target Words

refresh	unseat	dislike
reconsider	unfair	disrespect
reenter	uncover	discomfort
unhook		

Alternate Words

disgrace	undo	displease
reinstall	restart	reheat
untie	unbend	dismantle
reissue		

[Offline] ⏱ 15 minutes per day

Complete the Spelling activities with students. **For the full instructions for each activity, refer to pages SP 8–13.**

Day 1

Introduce Heart Words and Prefixes

[Materials]

- index cards (25)
- whiteboard (optional)

Advance Preparation

Write each Heart, Target, Challenge, and Alternate Word on a separate index card. Indicate on each card whether a word is a Heart, Target, Challenge, or Alternate Word.

Pretest

1. **Administer** a pretest using the Heart and Target Words.

2. **Gather** students' Words to Learn cards.

Note: If students didn't misspell any Heart, Target, Challenge, or Alternate Words, mark Lessons 2 and 3 complete and move to the online activity for Day 4 to practice for the Unit Checkpoint on Day 5.

Heart Words

⊃ *Skip this activity if students didn't misspell any Heart Words on this unit's pretest.*

1. **Gather** the Words to Learn cards for any Heart Words.

2. **Practice** the *new* Heart Words.

3. **Practice** *all* Heart Words.

4. **Track mastery** of Heart Words.

Target Words

⊃ *Skip this activity if students didn't misspell any Target Words on this unit's pretest.*

1. **Gather** the Words to Learn cards for any Target Words.

2. **Discover** the new spelling convention.

3. **Practice** the Target Words.

Challenge Words

⮑ *Skip this activity if students are struggling with the Heart Words and Target Words.*

1. **Gather** the Words to Learn cards for any Challenge Words.
2. **Discover** the new spelling convention in the Challenge Words.
3. **Practice** the Challenge Words.

Alternate Words

⮑ *Skip this activity if students don't have any Words to Learn cards for Alternate Words.*

1. **Gather** the Words to Learn cards for any Alternate Words.
2. **Discover** the new spelling convention in the Alternate Words.
3. **Practice** the Alternate Words.

Day 2 ....

Practice Spelling Words

Practice using the Activity Bank.

Day 3 ....

Practice Spelling Words

Practice using the Activity Bank.

 **minutes**

Day 4 ....

Review Spelling Words

Review using the online activity.

[Offline] **15** minutes

Day 5

Unit Checkpoint

1. **Dictate** the Words to Learn.

2. **Check** students' answers.

3. **Review** the words students misspelled.

Rewards:

- Help students find and play the online Spelling game, Spell 'n' Stack. Students should use levels 1–3.

- If students scored 80 percent or above on the Unit Checkpoint, add a sticker to the Unit 26 box on students' My Accomplishments chart. If students scored under 80 percent, continue to practice the words that they missed and add a sticker to this unit once they have mastered the words.

Heart Words and /l/ or /ul/ Spellings

Target spelling convention – **creating the /l/ or /ul/ sound with** *le* **or** *el*

Two common spellings for the sounds /l/ or /ul/ at the end of a word are *le* and *el*. Each of the Target Words in this unit ends with the sounds /l/ or /ul/ spelled *le* or *el*.

Unit Overview

	Offline	**15 minutes per day**
Day 1	Introduce Heart Words and /l/ or /ul/ Spellings	
Day 2	Practice Spelling Words	
Day 3	Practice Spelling Words	

	Online	**15 minutes**
Day 4	Review Spelling Words	

	Offline	**15 minutes**
Day 5	Unit Checkpoint	

♡ Heart Words

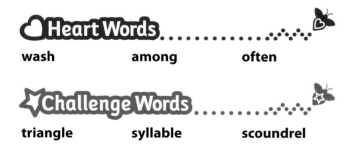

wash	among	often

✰ Challenge Words

triangle	syllable	scoundrel

◎ Target Words

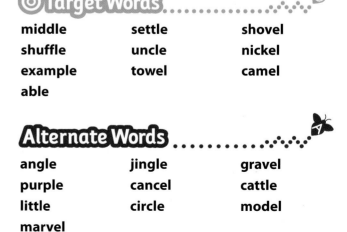

middle	settle	shovel
shuffle	uncle	nickel
example	towel	camel
able		

Alternate Words

angle	jingle	gravel
purple	cancel	cattle
little	circle	model
marvel		

 **Offline** 🕙 **minutes per day**

Complete the Spelling activities with students. **For the full instructions for each activity, refer to pages SP 8–13.**

Day 1 ....

Introduce Heart Words and /l/ or /ul/ Spellings

 **Materials**
- index cards (26)
- whiteboard (optional)

Advance Preparation

Write each Heart, Target, Challenge, and Alternate Word on a separate index card. Indicate on each card whether a word is a Heart, Target, Challenge, or Alternate Word.

Pretest

1. **Administer** a pretest using the Heart and Target Words.

2. **Gather** students' Words to Learn cards.

Note: If students didn't misspell any Heart, Target, Challenge, or Alternate Words, mark Lessons 2 and 3 complete and move to the online activity for Day 4 to practice for the Unit Checkpoint on Day 5.

Heart Words

➲ *Skip this activity if students didn't misspell any Heart Words on this unit's pretest.*

1. **Gather** the Words to Learn cards for any Heart Words.

2. **Practice** the *new* Heart Words.

3. **Practice** *all* Heart Words.

4. **Track mastery** of Heart Words.

Target Words

➲ *Skip this activity if students didn't misspell any Target Words on this unit's pretest.*

1. **Gather** the Words to Learn cards for any Target Words.

2. **Discover** the new spelling convention.

3. **Practice** the Target Words.

Challenge Words

↻ *Skip this activity if students are struggling with the Heart Words and Target Words.*

1. **Gather** the Words to Learn cards for any Challenge Words.
2. **Discover** the new spelling convention in the Challenge Words.
3. **Practice** the Challenge Words.

Alternate Words

↻ *Skip this activity if students don't have any Words to Learn cards for Alternate Words.*

1. **Gather** the Words to Learn cards for any Alternate Words.
2. **Discover** the new spelling convention in the Alternate Words.
3. **Practice** the Alternate Words.

Day 2

Practice Spelling Words

Practice using the Activity Bank.

Day 3

Practice Spelling Words

Practice using the Activity Bank.

 **15 minutes**

Day 4

Review Spelling Words

Review using the online activity.

[Offline] 🕔 minutes

Unit Checkpoint

1. **Dictate** the Words to Learn.

2. **Check** students' answers.

3. **Review** the words students misspelled.

 Rewards:

- Help students find and play the online Spelling game, Spell 'n' Stack. Students should use levels 1–3.

- If students scored 80 percent or above on the Unit Checkpoint, add a sticker to the Unit 27 box on students' My Accomplishments chart. If students scored under 80 percent, continue to practice the words that they missed and add a sticker to this unit once they have mastered the words.

Heart Words and *r*-Controlled Vowels

Target spelling convention — letter combinations that create the /ar/, /or/, and /ur/ sounds

The most common spelling for the sound /ar/ is *ar*. The most common spelling for the sound /or/ is *or*. The sound /ur/ can be spelled *or* or *ar*. Each of this unit's Target Words contains the sounds /ar/, /or/, or /ur/ spelled with one of these letter combinations.

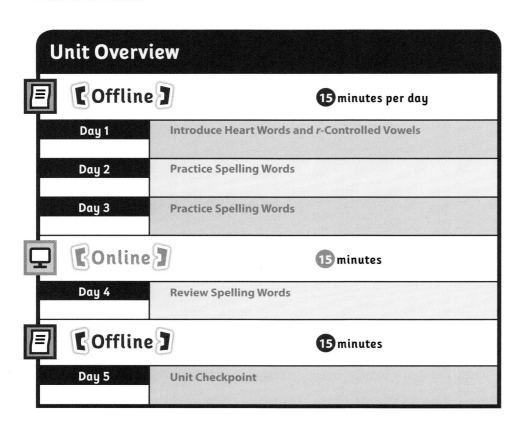

Unit Overview

[Offline]   15 minutes per day

Day 1	Introduce Heart Words and *r*-Controlled Vowels
Day 2	Practice Spelling Words
Day 3	Practice Spelling Words

[Online]   15 minutes

Day 4	Review Spelling Words

[Offline]   15 minutes

Day 5	Unit Checkpoint

Heart Words

your   island

Challenge Words

pharmacy   important   memorize

Target Words
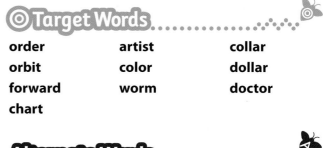

order	artist	collar
orbit	color	dollar
forward	worm	doctor
chart		

Alternate Words

born	march	alarm
work	upward	word
worn	yard	darling
backward		

[Offline] ⏱ **15** minutes per day

Complete the Spelling activities with students. **For the full instructions for each activity, refer to pages SP 8–13.**

Day 1 ....

Introduce Heart Words and *r*-Controlled Vowels

[Materials]

- index cards (25)
- whiteboard (optional)

Advance Preparation

Write each Heart, Target, Challenge, and Alternate Word on a separate index card. Indicate on each card whether a word is a Heart, Target, Challenge, or Alternate Word.

Pretest

1. **Administer** a pretest using the Heart and Target Words.

2. **Gather** students' Words to Learn cards.

Note: If students didn't misspell any Heart, Target, Challenge, or Alternate Words, mark Lessons 2 and 3 complete and move to the online activity for Day 4 to practice for the Unit Checkpoint on Day 5.

Heart Words

➲ *Skip this activity if students didn't misspell any Heart Words on this unit's pretest.*

1. **Gather** the Words to Learn cards for any Heart Words.

2. **Practice** the *new* Heart Words.

3. **Practice** *all* Heart Words.

4. **Track mastery** of Heart Words.

Target Words

➲ *Skip this activity if students didn't misspell any Target Words on this unit's pretest.*

1. **Gather** the Words to Learn cards for any Target Words.

2. **Discover** the new spelling convention.

3. **Practice** the Target Words.

Challenge Words

➲ *Skip this activity if students are struggling with the Heart Words and Target Words.*

1. **Gather** the Words to Learn cards for any Challenge Words.
2. **Discover** the new spelling convention in the Challenge Words.
3. **Practice** the Challenge Words.

Alternate Words

➲ *Skip this activity if students don't have any Words to Learn cards for Alternate Words.*

1. **Gather** the Words to Learn cards for any Alternate Words.
2. **Discover** the new spelling convention in the Alternate Words.
3. **Practice** the Alternate Words.

Day 2 ....

Practice Spelling Words

Practice using the Activity Bank.

Day 3 ....

Practice Spelling Words

Practice using the Activity Bank.

 **15 minutes**

Day 4 ....

Review Spelling Words

Review using the online activity.

[Offline] ⑮ minutes

Unit Checkpoint

1. **Dictate** the Words to Learn.

2. **Check** students' answers.

3. **Review** the words students misspelled.

Rewards:

- Help students find and play the online Spelling game, Spell 'n' Stack. Students should use levels 1–3.

- If students scored 80 percent or above on the Unit Checkpoint, add a sticker to the Unit 28 box on students' My Accomplishments chart. If students scored under 80 percent, continue to practice the words that they missed and add a sticker to this unit once they have mastered the words.

Heart Words and /aw/ Spellings

Target spelling convention — letter combinations that create the /aw/ sound

When the letter *a* is followed by two *l*'s, it almost always represents the /aw/ sound (*ball, fall, mall, call*). The three most common spellings for the sound /aw/ are *a, aw,* and *au*. Each of this unit's Target Words contains the sound /aw/ spelled with one of these letter combinations.

Objectives
• Spell Heart Words.
• Spell words containing the sound /aw/ spelled *a, aw,* or *au*.

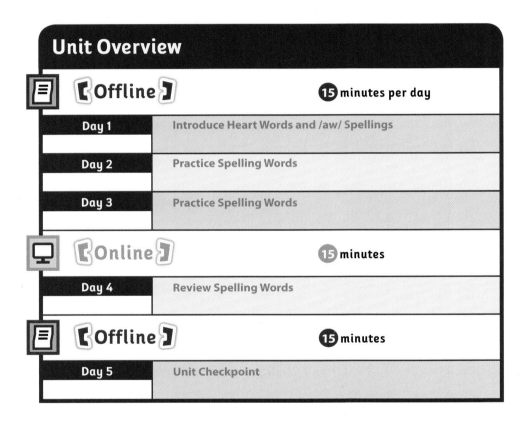

Unit Overview

📄 【Offline】 🕐 minutes per day

Day 1	Introduce Heart Words and /aw/ Spellings
Day 2	Practice Spelling Words
Day 3	Practice Spelling Words

🖥 【Online】 🕐 minutes

| Day 4 | Review Spelling Words |

📄 【Offline】 🕐 minutes

| Day 5 | Unit Checkpoint |

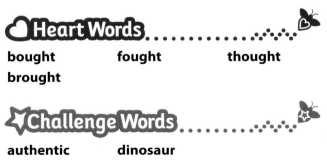

Heart Words

| bought | fought | thought |
| brought | | |

Challenge Words

| authentic | dinosaur |

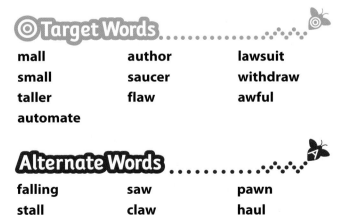

Target Words

mall	author	lawsuit
small	saucer	withdraw
taller	flaw	awful
automate		

Alternate Words

falling	saw	pawn
stall	claw	haul
ballpark	laundry	pause
hall		

[Offline] ⏱️ 15 minutes per day

Complete the Spelling activities with students. **For the full instructions for each activity, refer to pages SP 8–13.**

Day 1

Introduce Heart Words and /aw/ Spellings

[Materials]

- index cards (26)
- whiteboard (optional)

Advance Preparation

Write each Heart, Target, Challenge, and Alternate Word on a separate index card. Indicate on each card whether a word is a Heart, Target, Challenge, or Alternate Word.

Pretest

1. **Administer** a pretest using the Heart and Target Words.

2. **Gather** students' Words to Learn cards.

Note: If students didn't misspell any Heart, Target, Challenge, or Alternate Words, mark Lessons 2 and 3 complete and move to the online activity for Day 4 to practice for the Unit Checkpoint on Day 5.

Heart Words

➲ *Skip this activity if students didn't misspell any Heart Words on this unit's pretest.*

1. **Gather** the Words to Learn cards for any Heart Words.

2. **Practice** the *new* Heart Words.

3. **Practice** *all* Heart Words.

4. **Track mastery** of Heart Words.

Target Words

➲ *Skip this activity if students didn't misspell any Target Words on this unit's pretest.*

1. **Gather** the Words to Learn cards for any Target Words.

2. **Discover** the new spelling convention.

3. **Practice** the Target Words.

Challenge Words

↪ *Skip this activity if students are struggling with the Heart Words and Target Words.*

1. **Gather** the Words to Learn cards for any Challenge Words.
2. **Discover** the new spelling convention in the Challenge Words.
3. **Practice** the Challenge Words.

Alternate Words

↪ *Skip this activity if students don't have any Words to Learn cards for Alternate Words.*

1. **Gather** the Words to Learn cards for any Alternate Words.
2. **Discover** the new spelling convention in the Alternate Words.
3. **Practice** the Alternate Words.

Day 2

Practice Spelling Words

Practice using the Activity Bank.

Day 3

Practice Spelling Words

Practice using the Activity Bank.

 **15 minutes**

Day 4

Review Spelling Words

Review using the online activity.

〖 Offline 〗 ⏱ 15 minutes

Day 5

Unit Checkpoint

1. **Dictate** the Words to Learn.

2. **Check** students' answers.

3. **Review** the words students misspelled.

Rewards:

- Help students find and play the online Spelling game, Spell 'n' Stack. Students should use levels 1–3.

- If students scored 80 percent or above on the Unit Checkpoint, add a sticker to the Unit 29 box on students' My Accomplishments chart. If students scored under 80 percent, continue to practice the words that they missed and add a sticker to this unit once they have mastered the words.

Review Heart Words, Consonant Suffixes, Prefixes, /l/ & /ul/, r-Controlled Vowels, and /aw/

In this unit, students will review the spelling conventions and Heart Words they studied in the previous five units. Refer to the Unit Plans of previous units for a detailed description of each spelling convention.

Objectives

- Spell Heart Words.
- Spell words ending with consonant suffixes.
- Spell words beginning with the prefixes *re–*, *dis–*, or *un–*.
- Spell words containing the sounds /l/ or /ul/ spelled *le* or *el*.
- Spell words containing the sound /ar/ spelled *ar*.
- Spell words containing the sound /or/ spelled *or*.
- Spell words containing the sound /ur/ spelled *or* or *ar*.
- Spell words containing the sound /aw/ spelled *a*, *aw*, or *au*.

Unit Overview

📋 【Offline】 ⏱15 minutes per day

Day 1	Review Heart Words, Consonant Suffixes, Prefixes, /l/ & /ul/, r-Controlled Vowels, and /aw/
Day 2	Practice Spelling Words
Day 3	Practice Spelling Words

🖥 【Online】 ⏱15 minutes

| Day 4 | Review Spelling Words |

📋 【Offline】 ⏱15 minutes

| Day 5 | Unit Checkpoint |

☁ Heart Words

love	wash	bought
glove	among	brought
olive	often	fought
you	your	thought
half	island	

⭐ Challenge Words

recycle	harmless	unauthentic

◎ Target Words

quickly	uncle	color
dampness	towel	saucer
reenter	artist	flaw
unhook		

Alternate Words

wonderful	kettle	coverall
rewind	charm	

 **Offline** ⏱ **15 minutes per day**

Complete the Spelling activities with students. **For the full instructions for each activity, refer to pages SP 8–13.**

Day 1

Review Heart Words, Consonant Suffixes, Prefixes, /l/ & /ul/, r-Controlled Vowels, and /aw/

 **Materials**

- index cards (8)
- whiteboard (optional)

Advance Preparation

Gather the index cards you made previously for the Heart and Target Words listed. Write each Challenge and Alternate Word on a separate index card. Indicate on each card whether a word is a Challenge or Alternate Word.

Pretest

1. **Administer** a pretest using the Heart and Target Words.

2. **Gather** students' Words to Learn cards.

Note: If students didn't misspell any Heart, Target, Challenge, or Alternate Words, mark Lessons 2 and 3 complete and move to the online activity for Day 4 to practice for the Unit Checkpoint on Day 5.

Heart Words

➲ *Skip this activity if students didn't misspell any Heart Words on this unit's pretest.*

1. **Gather** the Words to Learn cards for any Heart Words.

2. **Practice** the Heart Words.

3. **Track mastery** of Heart Words.

Target Words

➲ *Skip this activity if students didn't misspell any Target Words on this unit's pretest.*

1. **Gather** the Words to Learn cards for any Target Words.

2. **Review** the previously studied spelling convention in each Target Word.

3. **Practice** the Target Words.

Challenge Words

⮌ *Skip this activity if students are struggling with the Heart Words and Target Words.*

1. **Gather** the Words to Learn cards for any Challenge Words.
2. **Review** the previously studied spelling convention in each Challenge Word.
3. **Practice** the Challenge Words.

Alternate Words

⮌ *Skip this activity if students don't have any Words to Learn cards for Alternate Words.*

1. **Gather** the Words to Learn cards for any Alternate Words.
2. **Review** the previously studied spelling convention in each Alternate Word.
3. **Practice** the Alternate Words.

Day 2 ....

Practice Spelling Words

Practice using the Activity Bank.

Day 3 ....

Practice Spelling Words

Practice using the Activity Bank.

 **15 minutes**

Day 4 ....

Review Spelling Words

Review using the online activity.

[Offline] 🕙 minutes

Day 5

Unit Checkpoint

1. **Dictate** the Words to Learn.

2. **Check** students' answers.

3. **Review** the words students misspelled.

Rewards:

- Help students find and play the online Spelling game, Spell 'n' Stack. Students should use levels 1–3.

- If students scored 80 percent or above on the Unit Checkpoint, add a sticker to the Unit 30 box on students' My Accomplishments chart. If students scored under 80 percent, continue to practice the words that they missed and add a sticker to this unit once they have mastered the words.

Heart Words and Long & Short Double *o* Spelled *oo*

Target spelling convention — using *oo* to create the long and the short double *o* sound

The letters *oo* can represent either the long double *o* sound, as in *moon*, or the short double *o* sound, as in *book*. Each of this unit's Target Words contains either the long double *o* sound or the short double *o* sound spelled with the letters *oo*.

Objectives
- Spell Heart Words.
- Spell words containing the long double *o* sound spelled *oo*.
- Spell words containing the short double *o* sound spelled *oo*.

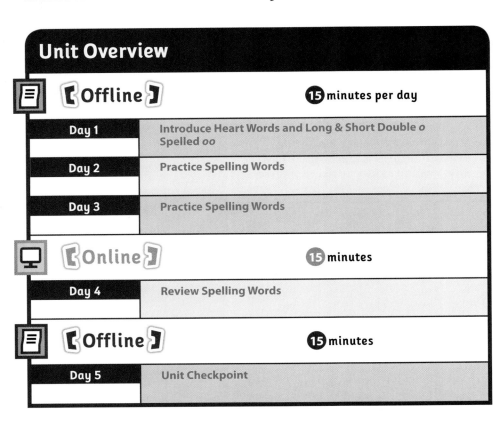

Unit Overview

	【Offline】	**15** minutes per day
Day 1	Introduce Heart Words and Long & Short Double *o* Spelled *oo*	
Day 2	Practice Spelling Words	
Day 3	Practice Spelling Words	

	【Online】	**15** minutes
Day 4	Review Spelling Words	

	【Offline】	**15** minutes
Day 5	Unit Checkpoint	

Heart Words

second   who   whole
was

Challenge Words

tenderfoot   afternoon   tablespoon

Target Words

stood	woodwork	groom
goodwill	undertook	tool
took	food	soon
hook		

Alternate Words

scrooge	gloom	cookbook
outlook	fishhook	bathroom
choose	moonlight	spoon
workbook		

[Offline] ⏱ 15 minutes per day

Complete the Spelling activities with students. **For the full instructions for each activity, refer to pages SP 8–13.**

Day 1

Introduce Heart Words and Long & Short Double *o* Spelled *oo*

[**Materials**]

- **index cards (27)**
- **whiteboard (optional)**

Advance Preparation

Write each Heart, Target, Challenge, and Alternate Word on a separate index card. Indicate on each card whether a word is a Heart, Target, Challenge, or Alternate Word.

Pretest

1. **Administer** a pretest using the Heart and Target Words.

2. **Gather** students' Words to Learn cards.

Note: If students didn't misspell any Heart, Target, Challenge, or Alternate Words, mark Lessons 2 and 3 complete and move to the online activity for Day 4 to practice for the Unit Checkpoint on Day 5.

Heart Words

➲ *Skip this activity if students didn't misspell any Heart Words on this unit's pretest.*

1. **Gather** the Words to Learn cards for any Heart Words.

2. **Practice** the *new* Heart Words.

3. **Practice** *all* Heart Words.

4. **Track mastery** of Heart Words.

Target Words

➲ *Skip this activity if students didn't misspell any Target Words on this unit's pretest.*

1. **Gather** the Words to Learn cards for any Target Words.

2. **Discover** the new spelling convention.

3. **Practice** the Target Words.

Challenge Words

➲ *Skip this activity if students are struggling with the Heart Words and Target Words.*

1. **Gather** the Words to Learn cards for any Challenge Words.
2. **Discover** the new spelling convention in the Challenge Words.
3. **Practice** the Challenge Words.

Alternate Words

➲ *Skip this activity if students don't have any Words to Learn cards for Alternate Words.*

1. **Gather** the Words to Learn cards for any Alternate Words.
2. **Discover** the new spelling convention in the Alternate Words.
3. **Practice** the Alternate Words.

Day 2 ··

Practice Spelling Words

Practice using the Activity Bank.

Day 3 ··

Practice Spelling Words

Practice using the Activity Bank.

 15 minutes

Day 4 ··

Review Spelling Words

Review using the online activity.

[Offline] 🕐 minutes

Unit Checkpoint

1. **Dictate** the Words to Learn.

2. **Check** students' answers.

3. **Review** the words students misspelled.

Rewards:

- Help students find and play the online Spelling game, Spell 'n' Stack. Students should use levels 1–3.

- If students scored 80 percent or above on the Unit Checkpoint, add a sticker to the Unit 31 box on students' My Accomplishments chart. If students scored under 80 percent, continue to practice the words that they missed and add a sticker to this unit once they have mastered the words.

Heart Words and Suffix –*ed*

Target spelling convention – **base word + suffix –*ed***

The vowel suffix –*ed* can represent the sounds /ed/, /d/, and /t/. When adding a vowel suffix to a base word that ends in a silent *e*, the silent *e* is dropped. When adding a vowel suffix to a base word that ends in a single vowel followed by a consonant, the final consonant is doubled. Most other base words do not change spellings when a vowel suffix is added. Each of this unit's Target Words ends in the suffix –*ed*.

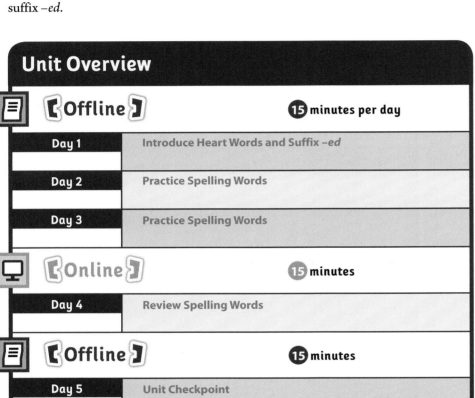

Unit Overview

Offline — 15 minutes per day

Day 1	Introduce Heart Words and Suffix –*ed*
Day 2	Practice Spelling Words
Day 3	Practice Spelling Words

Online — 15 minutes

| Day 4 | Review Spelling Words |

Offline — 15 minutes

| Day 5 | Unit Checkpoint |

Heart Words

| they | buy | young |
| goes | | |

Target Words

reached	behaved	honed
addressed	prepared	renamed
needed	clapped	glazed
blinked		

Challenge Words

| discovered | shivered | considered |

Alternate Words

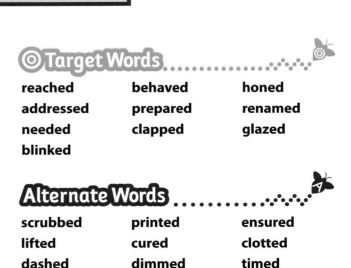

scrubbed	printed	ensured
lifted	cured	clotted
dashed	dimmed	timed
believed		

 **15** minutes per day

Complete the Spelling activities with students. **For the full instructions for each activity, refer to pages SP 8–13.**

Day 1

Introduce Heart Words and Suffix –ed

Materials

- index cards (27)
- whiteboard (optional)

Advance Preparation

Write each Heart, Target, Challenge, and Alternate Word on a separate index card. Indicate on each card whether a word is a Heart, Target, Challenge, or Alternate Word.

Pretest

1. **Administer** a pretest using the Heart and Target Words.

2. **Gather** students' Words to Learn cards.

Note: If students didn't misspell any Heart, Target, Challenge, or Alternate Words, mark Lessons 2 and 3 complete and move to the online activity for Day 4 to practice for the Unit Checkpoint on Day 5.

Heart Words

⮑ *Skip this activity if students didn't misspell any Heart Words on this unit's pretest.*

1. **Gather** the Words to Learn cards for any Heart Words.

2. **Practice** the *new* Heart Words.

3. **Practice** *all* Heart Words.

4. **Track mastery** of Heart Words.

Target Words

⮑ *Skip this activity if students didn't misspell any Target Words on this unit's pretest.*

1. **Gather** the Words to Learn cards for any Target Words.

2. **Discover** the new spelling convention.

3. **Practice** the Target Words.

Challenge Words

↪ *Skip this activity if students are struggling with the Heart Words and Target Words.*

1. **Gather** the Words to Learn cards for any Challenge Words.
2. **Discover** the new spelling convention in the Challenge Words.
3. **Practice** the Challenge Words.

Alternate Words

↪ *Skip this activity if students don't have any Words to Learn cards for Alternate Words.*

1. **Gather** the Words to Learn cards for any Alternate Words.
2. **Discover** the new spelling convention in the Alternate Words.
3. **Practice** the Alternate Words.

Day 2 ....

Practice Spelling Words

Practice using the Activity Bank.

Day 3 ....

Practice Spelling Words

Practice using the Activity Bank.

 **15 minutes**

Day 4 ....

Review Spelling Words

Review using the online activity.

【 Offline 】 ⓯ minutes

Unit Checkpoint

1. **Dictate** the Words to Learn.

2. **Check** students' answers.

3. **Review** the words students misspelled.

Rewards:

- Help students find and play the online Spelling game, Spell 'n' Stack. Students should use levels 1–3.

- If students scored 80 percent or above on the Unit Checkpoint, add a sticker to the Unit 32 box on students' My Accomplishments chart. If students scored under 80 percent, continue to practice the words that they missed and add a sticker to this unit once they have mastered the words.

Heart Words and Suffix *–ing*

Target spelling convention – **base word + suffix *–ing***

When adding a vowel suffix to a base word that ends in a silent *e*, the silent *e* is dropped. When adding a vowel suffix to a base word that ends in a single vowel followed by a consonant, the final consonant is doubled. Most other base words do not change spellings when a vowel suffix is added. Each of this unit's Target Words ends in the suffix *–ing*.

Objectives
- Spell Heart Words.
- Spell words ending in the vowel suffix *–ing*.

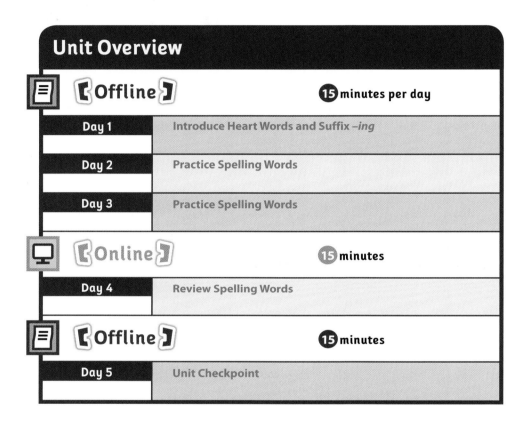

Unit Overview

Offline — 15 minutes per day

Day 1	Introduce Heart Words and Suffix *–ing*
Day 2	Practice Spelling Words
Day 3	Practice Spelling Words

Online — 15 minutes

| Day 4 | Review Spelling Words |

Offline — 15 minutes

| Day 5 | Unit Checkpoint |

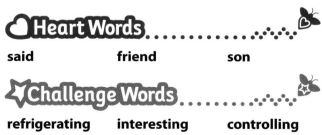

Heart Words

| said | friend | son |

Challenge Words

| refrigerating | interesting | controlling |

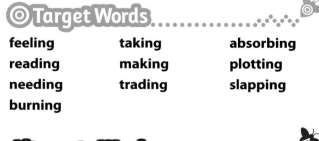

Target Words

feeling	taking	absorbing
reading	making	plotting
needing	trading	slapping
burning		

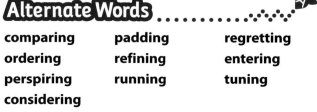

Alternate Words

comparing	padding	regretting
ordering	refining	entering
perspiring	running	tuning
considering		

[Offline] ⏱ minutes per day

Complete the Spelling activities with students. **For the full instructions for each activity, refer to pages SP 8–13.**

Day 1 ....

Introduce Heart Words and Suffix *–ing*

Materials

- index cards (26)
- whiteboard (optional)

Advance Preparation

Write each Heart, Target, Challenge, and Alternate Word on a separate index card. Indicate on each card whether a word is a Heart, Target, Challenge, or Alternate Word.

Pretest

1. **Administer** a pretest using the Heart and Target Words.

2. **Gather** students' Words to Learn cards.

Note: If students didn't misspell any Heart, Target, Challenge, or Alternate Words, mark Lessons 2 and 3 complete and move to the online activity for Day 4 to practice for the Unit Checkpoint on Day 5.

Heart Words

↻ *Skip this activity if students didn't misspell any Heart Words on this unit's pretest.*

1. **Gather** the Words to Learn cards for any Heart Words.

2. **Practice** the *new* Heart Words.

3. **Practice** *all* Heart Words.

4. **Track mastery** of Heart Words.

Target Words

↻ *Skip this activity if students didn't misspell any Target Words on this unit's pretest.*

1. **Gather** the Words to Learn cards for any Target Words.

2. **Discover** the new spelling convention.

3. **Practice** the Target Words.

Challenge Words

➲ *Skip this activity if students are struggling with the Heart Words and Target Words.*

1. **Gather** the Words to Learn cards for any Challenge Words.

2. **Discover** the new spelling convention in the Challenge Words.

3. **Practice** the Challenge Words.

Alternate Words

➲ *Skip this activity if students don't have any Words to Learn cards for Alternate Words.*

1. **Gather** the Words to Learn cards for any Alternate Words.

2. **Discover** the new spelling convention in the Alternate Words.

3. **Practice** the Alternate Words.

Day 2

Practice Spelling Words

Practice using the Activity Bank.

Day 3

Practice Spelling Words

Practice using the Activity Bank.

 **15 minutes**

Day 4

Review Spelling Words

Review using the online activity.

[Offline] ⏱ 15 minutes

Day 5

Unit Checkpoint

1. **Dictate** the Words to Learn.

2. **Check** students' answers.

3. **Review** the words students misspelled.

Rewards:

- Help students find and play the online Spelling game, Spell 'n' Stack. Students should use levels 1–3.

- If students scored 80 percent or above on the Unit Checkpoint, add a sticker to the Unit 33 box on students' My Accomplishments chart. If students scored under 80 percent, continue to practice the words that they missed and add a sticker to this unit once they have mastered the words.

Heart Words, Silent Consonants, Words Ending in *ic*, and Homophones

Target spelling convention — **using *wr* to make the /r/ sound; *kn* to make the /n/ sound, *ic* to make the /ĭk/ sound; spelling homophones**

The combination *wr* at the beginning of a word spells the sound /r/, *kn* at the beginning of a word spells the sound /n/, and *ic* at the end of words spells the sound /ĭk/. Homophones sound the same but have different spellings and meanings. Each of this unit's Target Words contains the letter combinations *wr*, *kn*, or *ic* or is a homophone.

Objectives
- Spell Heart Words.
- Spell words containing the letter combinations *wr* and *kn*.
- Spell words containing the sound /ĭk/ spelled *ic*.
- Spell homophones.

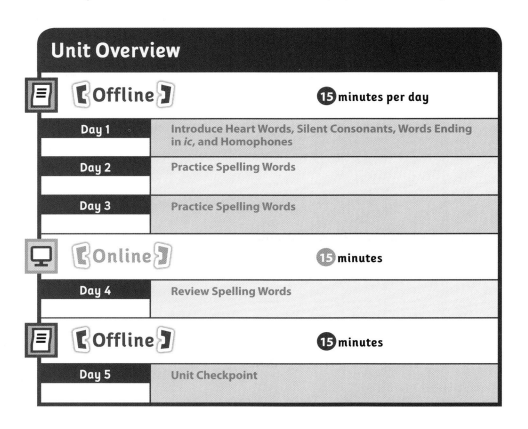

Unit Overview

	Offline		**15 minutes per day**
Day 1	Introduce Heart Words, Silent Consonants, Words Ending in *ic*, and Homophones		
Day 2	Practice Spelling Words		
Day 3	Practice Spelling Words		

	Online		**15 minutes**
Day 4	Review Spelling Words		

	Offline		**15 minutes**
Day 5	Unit Checkpoint		

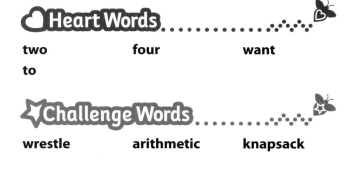

Heart Words

two	four	want
to		

Challenge Words

wrestle	arithmetic	knapsack

Target Words

traffic	wrong	night
magic	wrap	know
knee	knight	no
knock		

Alternate Words

knife	wrote	wreck
panic	electric	right
knuckle	write	wreath
elastic		

[Offline] 15 minutes per day

Complete the Spelling activities with students. **For the full instructions for each activity, refer to pages SP 8–13.**

Day 1 ....

Introduce Heart Words, Silent Consonants, Words Ending in *ic*, and Homophones

[Materials]

- index cards (27)
- whiteboard (optional)

Advance Preparation

Write each Heart, Target, Challenge, and Alternate Word on a separate index card. Indicate on each card whether a word is a Heart, Target, Challenge, or Alternate Word.

Pretest

1. **Administer** a pretest using the Heart and Target Words.

2. **Gather** students' Words to Learn cards.

Note: If students didn't misspell any Heart, Target, Challenge, or Alternate Words, mark Lessons 2 and 3 complete and move to the online activity for Day 4 to practice for the Unit Checkpoint on Day 5.

Heart Words

➲ *Skip this activity if students didn't misspell any Heart Words on this unit's pretest.*

1. **Gather** the Words to Learn cards for any Heart Words.

2. **Practice** the *new* Heart Words.

3. **Practice** *all* Heart Words.

4. **Track mastery** of Heart Words.

Target Words

➲ *Skip this activity if students didn't misspell any Target Words on this unit's pretest.*

1. **Gather** the Words to Learn cards for any Target Words.

2. **Discover** the new spelling convention.

3. **Practice** the Target Words.

Challenge Words

⮑ *Skip this activity if students are struggling with the Heart Words and Target Words.*

1. **Gather** the Words to Learn cards for any Challenge Words.
2. **Discover** the new spelling convention in the Challenge Words.
3. **Practice** the Challenge Words.

Alternate Words

⮑ *Skip this activity if students don't have any Words to Learn cards for Alternate Words.*

1. **Gather** the Words to Learn cards for any Alternate Words.
2. **Discover** the new spelling convention in the Alternate Words.
3. **Practice** the Alternate Words.

Day 2 ....

Practice Spelling Words

Practice using the Activity Bank.

Day 3 ....

Practice Spelling Words

Practice using the Activity Bank.

 **15 minutes**

Day 4 ....

Review Spelling Words

Review using the online activity.

〖Offline〗 ⏰ minutes

Unit Checkpoint

1. **Dictate** the Words to Learn.

2. **Check** students' answers.

3. **Review** the words students misspelled.

Rewards:

- Help students find and play the online Spelling game, Spell 'n' Stack. Students should use levels 1–3.

- If students scored 80 percent or above on the Unit Checkpoint, add a sticker to the Unit 34 box on students' My Accomplishments chart. If students scored under 80 percent, continue to practice the words that they missed and add a sticker to this unit once they have mastered the words.

Heart Words and Sounds of the *ea* Spelling

Target spelling convention – **sounds made by the letter combination *ea***

The long *a* sound, the long *e* sound, and the short *e* sound can all be spelled by the letter combination *ea*. Each of this unit's Target Words contains the letter combination *ea*.

> **Objectives**
> - Spell Heart Words.
> - Spell words containing the long *a* sound, the long *e* sound, or the short *e* sound spelled *ea*.

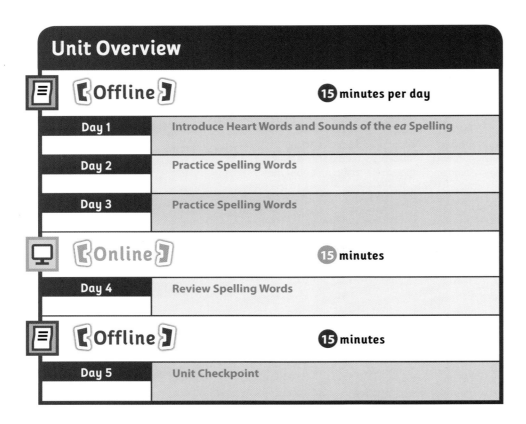

Unit Overview

📋 ❲Offline❳ — ⑮ minutes per day

Day 1	Introduce Heart Words and Sounds of the *ea* Spelling
Day 2	Practice Spelling Words
Day 3	Practice Spelling Words

💻 ❲Online❳ — ⑮ minutes

| Day 4 | Review Spelling Words |

📋 ❲Offline❳ — ⑮ minutes

| Day 5 | Unit Checkpoint |

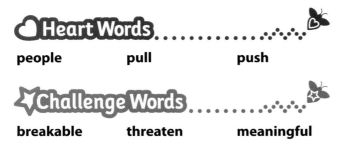

Heart Words

| people | pull | push |

Challenge Words

| breakable | threaten | meaningful |

Target Words

jeans	steak	thread
bean	break	spread
cream	great	death
team		

Alternate Words

cleaning	heavy	bear
instead	wear	weather
reader	feather	swear
already		

[Offline] ⏱ **15** minutes per day

Complete the Spelling activities with students. **For the full instructions for each activity, refer to pages SP 8–13.**

Day 1 ....

Introduce Heart Words and Sounds of the *ea* Spelling

[Materials]
- index cards (26)
- whiteboard (optional)

Advance Preparation

Write each Heart, Target, Challenge, and Alternate Word on a separate index card. Indicate on each card whether a word is a Heart, Target, Challenge, or Alternate Word.

Pretest

1. **Administer** a pretest using the Heart and Target Words.

2. **Gather** students' Words to Learn cards.

Note: If students didn't misspell any Heart, Target, Challenge, or Alternate Words, mark Lessons 2 and 3 complete and move to the online activity for Day 4 to practice for the Unit Checkpoint on Day 5.

Heart Words

➲ *Skip this activity if students didn't misspell any Heart Words on this unit's pretest.*

1. **Gather** the Words to Learn cards for any Heart Words.

2. **Practice** the *new* Heart Words.

3. **Practice** *all* Heart Words.

4. **Track mastery** of Heart Words.

Target Words

➲ *Skip this activity if students didn't misspell any Target Words on this unit's pretest.*

1. **Gather** the Words to Learn cards for any Target Words.

2. **Discover** the new spelling convention.

3. **Practice** the Target Words.

Challenge Words

➲ *Skip this activity if students are struggling with the Heart Words and Target Words.*

1. **Gather** the Words to Learn cards for any Challenge Words.
2. **Discover** the new spelling convention in the Challenge Words.
3. **Practice** the Challenge Words.

Alternate Words

➲ *Skip this activity if students don't have any Words to Learn cards for Alternate Words.*

1. **Gather** the Words to Learn cards for any Alternate Words.
2. **Discover** the new spelling convention in the Alternate Words.
3. **Practice** the Alternate Words.

Day 2

Practice Spelling Words

Practice using the Activity Bank.

Day 3

Practice Spelling Words

Practice using the Activity Bank.

 **15** minutes

Day 4

Review Spelling Words

Review using the online activity.

[Offline] **15** minutes

Day 5

Unit Checkpoint

1. **Dictate** the Words to Learn.

2. **Check** students' answers.

3. **Review** the words students misspelled.

Rewards:

- Help students find and play the online Spelling game, Spell 'n' Stack. Students should use levels 1–3.

- If students scored 80 percent or above on the Unit Checkpoint, add a sticker to the Unit 35 box on students' My Accomplishments chart. If students scored under 80 percent, continue to practice the words that they missed and add a sticker to this unit once they have mastered the words.

Review Heart Words, *oo*, Suffixes *−ed* & *−ing*, Silent Consonants, Homophones, *ic*, and *ea*

In this unit, students will review the spelling conventions and Heart Words they studied in the previous five units. Refer to the Unit Plans of previous units for a detailed description of each spelling convention.

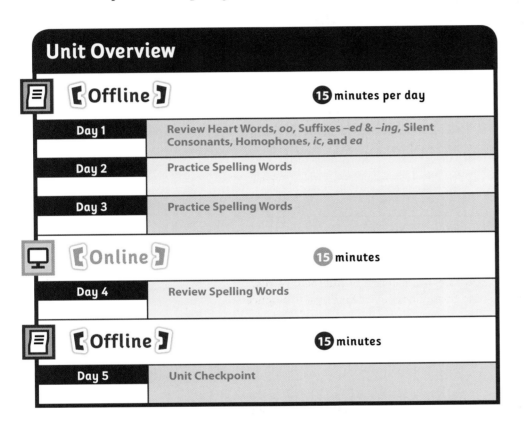

Unit Overview

Offline — 15 minutes per day

Day 1	Review Heart Words, *oo*, Suffixes *−ed* & *−ing*, Silent Consonants, Homophones, *ic*, and *ea*
Day 2	Practice Spelling Words
Day 3	Practice Spelling Words

Online — 15 minutes

| Day 4 | Review Spelling Words |

Offline — 15 minutes

| Day 5 | Unit Checkpoint |

Heart Words

young	goes	to
second	buy	four
was	said	want
who	friend	people
whole	son	pull
they	two	push

Target Words

took	plotting	wrong
food	trading	bean
behaved	knee	thread
clapped		

Alternate Words

loom	capping	dread
primed	knead	

Challenge Words

shooting	defeated	knighted

[Offline] ⏱ **15** minutes per day

Complete the Spelling activities with students. **For the full instructions for each activity, refer to pages SP 8–13.**

Day 1 ....

Review Heart Words, *oo*, Suffixes *–ed* & *–ing*, Silent Consonants, Homophones, *ic*, and *ea*

[Materials]

- index cards (8)
- whiteboard (optional)

Advance Preparation

Gather the index cards you made previously for the Heart and Target Words listed. Write each Challenge and Alternate Word on a separate index card. Indicate on each card whether a word is a Challenge or Alternate Word.

Pretest

1. **Administer** a pretest using the Heart and Target Words.

2. **Gather** students' Words to Learn cards.

Note: If students didn't misspell any Heart, Target, Challenge, or Alternate Words, mark Lessons 2 and 3 complete and move to the online activity for Day 4 to practice for the Unit Checkpoint on Day 5.

Heart Words

➲ *Skip this activity if students didn't misspell any Heart Words on this unit's pretest.*

1. **Gather** the Words to Learn cards for any Heart Words.

2. **Practice** the Heart Words.

3. **Track mastery** of Heart Words.

Target Words

➲ *Skip this activity if students didn't misspell any Target Words on this unit's pretest.*

1. **Gather** the Words to Learn cards for any Target Words.

2. **Review** the previously studied spelling convention in each Target Word.

3. **Practice** the Target Words.

Challenge Words

➲ *Skip this activity if students are struggling with the Heart Words and Target Words.*

1. **Gather** the Words to Learn cards for any Challenge Words.
2. **Review** the previously studied spelling convention in each Challenge Word.
3. **Practice** the Challenge Words.

Alternate Words

➲ *Skip this activity if students don't have any Words to Learn cards for Alternate Words.*

1. **Gather** the Words to Learn cards for any Alternate Words.
2. **Review** the previously studied spelling convention in each Alternate Word.
3. **Practice** the Alternate Words.

Day 2 ....

Practice Spelling Words

Practice using the Activity Bank.

Day 3 ....

Practice Spelling Words

Practice using the Activity Bank.

 **15** minutes

Day 4 ....

Review Spelling Words

Review using the online activity.

[Offline] ⓯ minutes

Unit Checkpoint

1. **Dictate** the Words to Learn.

2. **Check** students' answers.

3. **Review** the words students misspelled.

Rewards:

- Help students find and play the online Spelling game, Spell 'n' Stack. Students should use levels 1–3.

- If students scored 80 percent or above on the Unit Checkpoint, add a sticker to the Unit 36 box on students' My Accomplishments chart. If students scored under 80 percent, continue to practice the words that they missed and add a sticker to this unit once they have mastered the words.

Spelling Activity Bank

Vowel-Free Words

1. Say each of the Words to Learn to students. Have students write only the consonants in each word and put a dot where each vowel belongs.

2. Have students tell you which vowels should be in the places they wrote dots.

3. Note any words that students spelled incorrectly, and correct the spelling errors with students.

Spelling Memory

1. Ask students to write as many of the Words to Learn as they can remember on a sheet of paper.

2. When students finish, remind them of any words they forgot and have them complete the list.

3. Note any words that students spelled incorrectly, and correct the spelling errors with students.

Fill In the Blank

1. Write a sentence that uses one of the Words to Learn, but leave a blank space where that word would go in the sentence.

2. Ask students to fill in the correct word to complete the sentence. Sometimes more than one word will correctly complete a sentence.

3. Repeat with each of the Words to Learn.

4. Note any words that students spelled incorrectly, and correct the spelling errors with students.

Silly Sentences

1. Ask students to write a silly sentence using each of the Words to Learn.

2. Have students underline the word in each of their sentences.
   Sample sentence: *The <u>dog</u> was driving a car.*

3. Note any words that students spelled incorrectly, and correct the spelling errors with students.

Spelling Baseball

1. Draw a baseball diamond with four bases (see example).

2. Tell students that you are the pitcher and they are the batter.

3. Choose a word from the Words to Learn and ask students to spell it.

   ▸ If students spell the word correctly, they get to move one base.
   ▸ If the students spell the word wrong, that is one strike.
   ▸ If students get three strikes on the same word, that is one out.
   ▸ If students spell four words correctly, they have moved around all four bases. They score a run (one point)!

4. Continue giving students words until each of the Words to Learn has been used. See how many points students can earn.

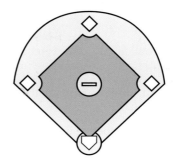

Spelling Story

Have students write a very short story using as many of the Words to Learn as they can.

Which Is Correct?

1. Write out three versions of one of the Words to Learn, spelling two versions incorrectly and one correctly.

2. Have students pick out which of the versions is correct and write the correct spelling of the word.

Alphabetize

1. Have students write the Words to Learn in alphabetical order.

2. Note any words that students spelled incorrectly, and correct the spelling errors with students.

Guess the Word

1. While students are looking at the Words to Learn, say any letter from one of the words. Ask students to guess which word you are thinking of.

2. Say a second letter in the word, a third, and so on until students correctly guess your word.

3. After students guess the word, have them spell that word aloud.

4. Repeat the activity with several words.

Guess the Word Reversed

1. While students are looking at the Words to Learn, have them say any letter from one of the words. Try to guess which word students are thinking of.

2. Have students say a second letter in the word, a third, and so on until you correctly guess the word.

3. After you guess the word, have students spell that word aloud.

4. Repeat the activity with several words.

Hidden Picture

1. Have students draw a picture and "hide" as many of the Words to Learn as they can inside the picture.

2. See if you or others can find the words within the picture.
(The example has the spelling words *can*, *fix*, *fun*, and *red* hidden in the picture.)

3. Note any words that students spelled incorrectly, and correct the spelling errors with students.

Word Scramble

1. Write the letters of each of the Words to Learn in scrambled order.

2. Have students write the correctly spelled word next to each of your scrambled words.

Rhymes

1. Have students write each of the Words to Learn.

2. Next to each word, have them write a rhyming word.

3. If there is time, have students try to come up with more than one rhyming word for some of the Words to Learn.

TIP Students may come across rhyming words that are from different word families and are spelled with different spelling conventions (such as *half* and *laugh*). These are valid rhymes, but you should discuss the differences in the spellings with students.

Rhymes Reversed

1. For each of the Words to Learn, write a word that rhymes with it on a piece of paper and then leave a space blank.

2. In the blank, have students fill in the word that rhymes with the word you wrote.

3. Note any words that students spelled incorrectly, and correct the spelling errors with students.

TIP Do not include rhyming words that are from different word families and are spelled with different spelling conventions (such as *half* and *laugh*). These are valid rhymes, but the differences in spelling can be confusing to students.

Crosswords

1. Have students write one of the Words to Learn in the center of a sheet of paper.

2. Have them write another of the Words to Learn by going across and sharing a letter with the first word. See how many words students can connect.

```
                    p
            k  i  s  s  e  s
         d           n
      r  o  c  k  s
         g
         s
```

Roll the Number Cube

1. Have students roll the number cube.

2. Have students write one of the Words to Learn the number of times indicated by their roll.

3. Continue the process, having students roll the cube and write a word that many times, until they've written all the Words to Learn.

4. Note any words that students spelled incorrectly, and correct the spelling errors with students.

Materials

- household objects – six-sided number cube (labeled 1 through 6)

Snowman

1. Draw a snowman with three circles for the body and head, two eyes, a nose, and hands (see example).

2. Pick one of the Words to Learn, but do not tell students which word you have chosen.

3. Draw one blank space under the snowman for each letter of the word.

4. Ask students to guess what letters might be in the word you have chosen.

5. Each time students make an incorrect guess, erase one part of the snowman. The object of the game is for students to try and guess the whole word before the snowman melts.

__ __ __ __ __

Spelling Search

1. Have students search for each of the Words to Learn in newspapers, books, or magazines.

2. Have them write down each word as they find it.

Word Search Puzzle

1. Draw a large box on a piece of lined paper or graph paper.

2. Fill in the box with Words to Learn, writing them horizontally, vertically, and diagonally (forward or backward if you choose).

3. Fill in the rest of the box with random letters.

4. After giving students a list of this unit's words, have them find and circle the words in the puzzle.

Quickfire

1. Tell students to write down each word you say as quickly as they can. Warn them, however, that misspellings come with a 10-second penalty.

2. Time how long it takes students to write all the Words to Learn after you say them.

3. Check students' lists for misspellings, adding 10 seconds for each mistake.

4. Encourage students to try again to improve their time.

5. After two or more attempts, note any words that students spelled incorrectly, and correct the spelling errors with students.

[Materials]

- household objects (optional) – newspaper, book, magazine

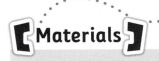

[Materials]

- household objects – a watch with a second hand

Pictionary/Charades

1. Draw or act out something to make students guess one of the Words to Learn.

2. When students guess correctly, have them write the word down.

3. Repeat the activity with several words.

4. Note any words that students spelled incorrectly, and correct the spelling errors with students.

Mnemonics

1. Have students write one of the Words to Learn vertically.

2. Check that students have spelled the word correctly.

3. Have students write words beginning with each letter of the vertical word horizontally.

4. Encourage students to say the vertical word, then the horizontal words, and then the vertical word again.

w	e		
a	l	l	
l	o	v	e
k	i	t	e	s

Mnemonics Reversed

1. Come up with a mnemonic for one of the Words to Learn.

2. Say the mnemonic for students, explaining that the first letters of each word you said combine to spell one of the Words to Learn.

3. Have students spell the word based on your mnemonic.

4. Repeat for each of the Words to Learn.

5. Note any words that students spelled incorrectly, and correct the spelling errors with students.

Example: **walk**
You say: **"We all love kites"**
Students write: **"w-a-l-k"**

Spelling Tennis

1. Tell a student that the two of you are going to play spelling tennis, and that the way you will "hit" the ball to each other is by saying the right letter as you spell a word.

[Materials]

- household objects – tennis ball

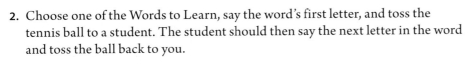

2. Choose one of the Words to Learn, say the word's first letter, and toss the tennis ball to a student. The student should then say the next letter in the word and toss the ball back to you.

   ▸ If the student names the correct letter, it is your turn to add a letter and throw the ball back.
   ▸ If the student names an incorrect letter, you get a point.
   ▸ If the student reaches the end of a word without making any mistakes, he or she gets a point.
   ▸ The first person to get four points wins the game.

3. Continue spelling words like this, alternating who begins (who "serves"), until each of the Words to Learn has been used. See how many points students can earn.

4. Note any words that students spell incorrectly, and correct the spelling errors with students.

TIP If students are familiar with tennis terminology and scoring, use it to make the game more fun. If a student finishes the first word without making any mistakes, the score would be Love-15.

Musical Spelling

1. Tell students that this game works like Musical Chairs.

2. Give them a list of the Words to Learn and tell them that, for as long as the music plays, they must copy as many words as possible onto a new sheet of paper.

3. Explain that they will get one point for each word they spell correctly, but warn them that they will lose one point for every incorrectly spelled word.

4. Play the music and let students begin copying words.

5. After you stop the music, check student papers for errors and tally up their score.

6. Note any words that students spelled incorrectly, and correct the spelling errors with students.

Materials

- household objects – music, music player

Code Words

Sample Key: a = 1, b = 2, c = 3, d = 4, etc.

1. Use the key to translate each of the Words to Learn into a series of numbers. Write down the translations on a piece of paper.

2. Give students the key and the paper with the translations on it.

Example:
3–1–20 = *cat*
4–15–7 = *dog*

3. Have students use the key to decode each series of numbers on the paper.

4. After students decode each series of numbers, check their spellings.

5. Note any words that students spelled incorrectly, and correct the spelling errors with students.

Materials

- a key that lists and numbers the letters of the alphabet, in order, from 1 to 26

Bingo!

[Materials]

- household objects –
  bingo card, five columns
  intersected by five rows,
  with the middle square
  labeled "Free" and the
  columns headed B-I-N-G-O;
  15–20 pennies

1. Have students fill in the 24 open squares on the bingo card with Words to Learn as you read the words aloud. Students should write each word in any empty box they choose and need not fill up their card in any set order.

2. Once all 24 squares are filled in, check for misspellings.

3. Note any words that students spelled incorrectly, and correct the spelling errors with students.

4. Then give students the pennies and explain to them that, when they hear a word, they must find it on their card and cover it with a penny. Tell them that the game is over when they have five squares in a row covered and they yell, "Bingo!"

5. In random order, read the Words to Learn aloud again.

6. After students yell, "Bingo!" check their cards to make sure they covered the appropriate words.